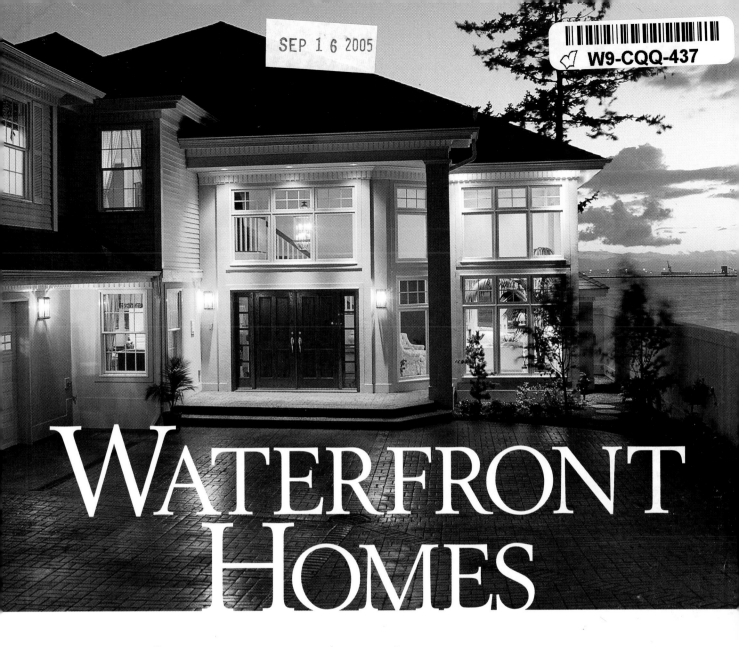

WATERFRONT HOMES

189 HOME PLANS *for River, Lake or Sea*

WATERFRONT HOMES

Second Edition

Published by Home Planners, LLC
Wholly Owned by Hanley-Wood, LLC
One Thomas Circle, NW, Suite 600
Washington, DC 20005

Distribution Center
29333 Lorie Lane
Wixom, Michigan 48393

Group Vice President, General Manager, Andrew Schultz
Vice President, Publishing, Jennifer Pearce
Executive Editor, Linda Bellamy
Managing Editor, Jason D. Vaughan
Editor, Nate Ewell
Associate Editor, Simon Hyoun
Lead Plan Merchandiser, Morenci C. Clark
Plan Merchandiser, Nicole Phipps
Proofreader/Copywriter, Dyana Weis
Graphic Artist, Joong Min
Plan Data Team Leader, Ryan Emge
Production Manager, Brenda McClary

Vice President, Retail Sales, Scott Hill
National Sales Manager, Bruce Holmes
Director, Plan Products, Matt Higgins

For direct sales, contact Retail Vision at (800) 381-1288 ext 6053

BIG DESIGNS, INC.

President, Creative Director, Anthony D'Elia
Vice President, Business Manager, Megan D'Elia
Vice President, Design Director, Chris Bonavita
Editorial Director, John Roach
Assistant Editor, Tricia Starkey
Senior Art Director, Stephen Reinfurt
Production Director, David Barbella
Photo Editor, Christine DiVuolo
Art Director, Jessica Hagenbuch
Graphic Designer, Mary Ellen Mulshine
Graphic Designer, Lindsey O'Neill-Myers
Graphic Designer, Jacque Young
Assistant Photo Editor, Brian Wilson
Assistant Production Manager, Rich Fuentes

PHOTO CREDITS

Front Cover Top: Design HPK0200010.
Photo by Bri Mar Photography.
See page 17 for details.
Front Cover Lower Left and Right: Photos by Sam Gray.
Back Cover: Design HPK0200015. ©1994 Donald A. Gardner Architects, Inc.,
Photography courtesy of Donald A. Gardner Architects, Inc.
See page 22 for details.
Facing Page Top: Chris A. Little of Atlanta
Facing Page Lower Left: Photo courtesy of: William E. Poole Designs, Inc.
Facing Page Lower Right: ©1998 Donald A. Gardner, Inc.,
Photography courtesy of Donald A. Gardner Architects, Inc.

10 9 8 7 6 5 4 3 2 1

Printed in the United States of America
Library of Congress Control Number: 2004106184

ISBN #: 1-931131-28-7

WATERFRONT HOMES

8

9

10

ON THE WATER

Anyone who has listened to a CD filled with the soothing sounds of lake or ocean waves knows the calming effects of life by the water.

Maybe that's what inspired you to build your own home by a lake, river, or sea. Or perhaps it's the sights you can enjoy from the coast, more than the sounds, that drew you in.

All of those reasons help explain why waterfront living has always had a special allure. In the Romantic Period, writers and painters like Thoreau chose the point where the water meets the land as a frequent subject of their writing or artwork. To this day, it has a captivating quality to it. Moment to moment, day to day, the coastline offers an ever-changing landscape—it never looks exactly the same, no matter how often you look at it.

THIS PRIVATE THIRD-FLOOR BALCONY
PROVIDES THE BEST VIEWS IN THE HOUSE.

On the curved deck off the living room, teak steamer chairs provide a place to relax and enjoy the spectacular views of Puget Sound.

Combine that sense of beauty and mystery with the cool breezes and restorative qualities of life by the water, and it's no surprise that waterfront homes have always been a favorite vacation spot. A growing number of people are turning to waterfront regions for all-year living, instead of just seasonal retreats.

Whether you are looking for a vacation get-away, year-round home, or retirement paradise, this collection of 189 beautiful home plans can help you find the home that will fulfill all your dreams of living on the water's edge.

SECRETS OF WATERFRONT DESIGN

The focus of any great waterfront home should be its surroundings, not the home itself. That's not achieved by simply building a Spartan home, however. From the inside, the best waterfront homes have all the luxuries and amenities you can imagine, while maintaining an appreciation for the natural beauty around them.

Unlike a traditional home—where curb appeal is a valuable buzzword—waterfront homes need to fit with their surroundings whether they are approached by land or sea. With the home's "focus" typically directed towards the water, this can present a particular design challenge for the approach by car or on foot. The best of these homes mesh with the landscape naturally from every angle—even brand-new, contemporary houses can fit seamlessly with their surroundings with the right design.

Playing off this appreciation for your surroundings is the importance of outdoor living spaces in a waterfront home. Whether it's a porch, deck, patio, lanai, or some combination of

ON THE WATER

these, the views along the coast lure people outside, providing an easy transition from indoors to out, and vice versa. These spaces can accommodate outdoor dining, sunbathing, or simply relaxing in a hammock with a good book.

Adding a screened porch can be an attractive option, especially near the kitchen for outdoor meals. Screened porches can be peaceful, relaxing alternatives in the evening after a day spent sunbathing on an open-air deck or lounging in the water.

Keep the water views in mind as you move inside as well. Look for a design that will suit your property, and your lifestyle. You'll want the home's central gathering room—probably its great room or family room—to enjoy views of the water, preferably through large, expansive windows. Other spaces you use frequently should "face out," if possible, as well. Large windows in the master bedroom that overlook the water will help you welcome the day and enjoy the soothing sounds of waves at night. If you love to cook, look for a kitchen that has a large window above the sink, or a bay window in the adjacent breakfast area.

Special design touches can add to the allure of the water as well. Create an unobstructed view from your foyer to a window overlooking the water, and visitors will be naturally drawn into your home as soon as they arrive.

This covered porch is the perfect spot for morning coffee or an afternoon nap. For details on design HPK0200010, turn to page 17.

PLANNING FOR YOUR YEAR-ROUND GETAWAY

A growing number of waterfront homeowners use their homes for more than just a summer vacation spot. If that's the case for you, there are some special considerations you'll want to keep in mind—and they are worth thinking about even if you aren't ready to live in your waterfront home year-round, but may want to eventually.

Since many waterfront locations are in remote areas, you could have a big commute ahead of you if you live there year-round. Be prepared for that travel, or be sure to equip your home with the technology you would need to telecommute, if that's a possibility. You may also want to include satellite television; roughing it may be nice for a summer weekend, but can get old if it's for months on end.

Get to know the off-season climate, too, before you break ground. Land that stays dry during the summer may have a damp rainy season. Local builders and contractors will be able to help you ensure that you are on solid ground. The winter weather may surprise you,

too, if you haven't spent time there before. Waterfront property may seem colder and more remote than you might expect when the winter wind whips off the water.

> "A lake is the landscape's most beautiful and expressive feature. It is earth's eye; looking into which the beholder measures the depth of his own nature."
>
> — Henry David Thoreau

PLANNING YOUR VACATION HOME

While many of us would love to spend the rest of our days in our waterfront retreat, it's still a long ways off for most homebuilders. If your waterfront home will serve as a vacation spot for you and your family—at least for the foreseeable future—there is another set of unique considerations to keep in mind.

First, you'll want to build your vacation home in a location that is easily accessible. You'll find this convenient during the building process—you don't want to be completely out of touch during construction—but even more valuable in the future. Ideally, you want to allow for the possibility of hopping in the car on a Friday afternoon and getting there with time to enjoy the weekend.

Second, you don't want to build a vacation retreat simply for investment's sake. Historically, they haven't performed as well in terms of resale as you might expect, and renting the home when it's not in use can be more trouble than it's worth. If you plan to build, build for you and your family's enjoyment—not for the possibility of a financial windfall.

Finally, and most importantly, make a list of what you and your family hope to gain from your waterfront home. Is it simply a place to relax and get away from it all? How important are life's creature comforts at your getaway? Are fishing, boating, or other water sports priorities?

Answers to those questions will help you create the perfect waterfront home, whether it's just a weekend escape or a year-round residence. ∎

TOP: A DIMINUTIVE BALCONY OUTSIDE THE PALLADIAN-STYLE FRENCH DOORS IS JUST BIG ENOUGH FOR TWO. ABOVE: A SCREENED PORCH CAN BE A PERFECT SETTING FOR A TRANSITION BETWEEN INDOORS AND OUT. RIGHT: A TURRET ADDS A FLAIR TO THIS LAKEFRONT WRAPAROUND PORCH.

SEA BREEZE
CAPTURE THE SPIRIT OF WATERFRONT LIVING

PHOTOS BY CHRIS A. LITTLE OF ATLANTA

THIS HOME, AS SHOWN IN THE PHOTOGRAPH, MAY DIFFER FROM THE ACTUAL BLUEPRINTS. FOR MORE DETAILED INFORMATION, PLEASE CHECK THE FLOOR PLANS CAREFULLY.

plan# HPK0200001

STYLE: SEASIDE
FIRST FLOOR: 1,122 SQ. FT.
SECOND FLOOR: 528 SQ. FT.
TOTAL: 1,650 SQ. FT.
BEDROOMS: 4
BATHROOMS: 2
WIDTH: 34' - 0"
DEPTH: 52' - 5"
FOUNDATION: PIER

SEARCH ONLINE @ EPLANS.COM

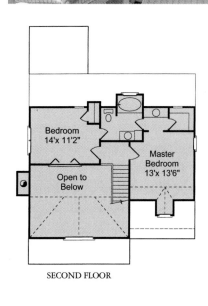

This lovely seaside vacation home is perfect for seasonal family getaways or for the family that lives coastal year round. The spacious front deck is great for private sunbathing or outdoor barbecues, providing breathtaking ocean views. The two-story living room is warmed by a fireplace on breezy beach nights, while the island kitchen overlooks the open dining area nearby. Two first-floor family bedrooms share a hall bath. Upstairs, the master bedroom features a walk-in closet, dressing area with a vanity and access to a whirlpool tub shared with an additional family bedroom.

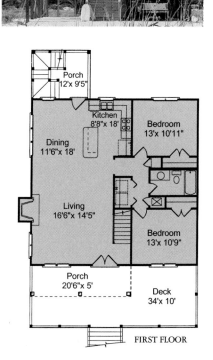

Porch
12'x 9'5"

Kitchen
8'8"x 18'

Dining
11'6"x 18'

Bedroom
13'x 10'11"

Living
16'6"x 14'5"

Bedroom
13'x 10'9"

Porch
20'6"x 5'

Deck
34'x 10'

FIRST FLOOR

Bedroom
14'x 11'2"

Master
Bedroom
13'x 13'6"

Open to
Below

SECOND FLOOR

CLASSIC CHARM
GRAB A SPOT ON THE PORCH AND ENJOY THE VIEW

plan# HPK0200002

STYLE: COLONIAL
FIRST FLOOR: 3,016 SQ. FT.
SECOND FLOOR: 1,283 SQ. FT.
TOTAL: 4,299 SQ. FT.
BONUS SPACE: 757 SQ. FT.
BEDROOMS: 4
BATHROOMS: 4½ + ½
WIDTH: 105' - 0"
DEPTH: 69' - 0"
FOUNDATION: CRAWLSPACE

SEARCH ONLINE @ EPLANS.COM

SECOND FLOOR

FIRST FLOOR

With 10-foot wood-beam ceilings on the first floor and nine-foot ceilings upstairs, this Dutch Colonial offers plenty of aesthetic appeal. Enter the foyer to a dining room with an arched entrance on the left, and to the right, a living room/library with transom pocket doors and a fireplace. The kitchen is full of modern amenities, including an island with a vegetable sink and a snack bar. The master wing provides peace and quiet— and a few surprises! Details like a window seat, whirlpool tub, and storage space make it a welcome retreat. Upstairs, three bedroom suites, each with private baths, offer room for family and guests. Future space is available for expansion.

A GREAT ESCAPE
ENJOY A RUSTIC APPEAL WITH ALL THE AMENITIES

plan# HPK0200003

STYLE: CRAFTSMAN
MAIN LEVEL: 3,040 SQ. FT.
LOWER LEVEL: 1,736 SQ. FT.
TOTAL: 4,776 SQ. FT.
BEDROOMS: 5
BATHROOMS: 4½ + ½
DEPTH: 104' - 2"

SEARCH ONLINE @ EPLANS.COM

Looking a bit like a mountain resort, this fine Rustic-style home is sure to be the envy of your neighborhood. Entering through the elegant front door, one finds an open staircase to the right and a spacious great room directly ahead. Here, a fireplace and a wall of windows give a cozy welcome. A lavish master suite begins with a sitting room complete with a fireplace and continues to a private porch, large walk-in closet, and sumptuous bedroom area. The gourmet kitchen adjoins a sunny dining room that offers access to a screened porch.

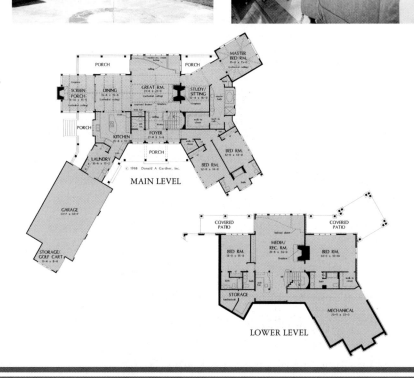

MAIN LEVEL

LOWER LEVEL

HIGH TIDE
BEST-SELLING WATERFRONT HOMES IN FULL COLOR

REAR EXTERIOR

plan# HPK0200004

STYLE: SEASIDE
FIRST FLOOR: 1,552 SQ. FT.
SECOND FLOOR: 653 SQ. FT.
TOTAL: 2,205 SQ. FT.
BEDROOMS: 3
BATHROOMS: 2
WIDTH: 60' - 0"
DEPTH: 50' - 0"
FOUNDATION: PIER

SEARCH ONLINE @ EPLANS.COM

A split staircase adds flair to this European-style coastal home, where a fireplace brings warmth on chilly evenings. The foyer opens to the expansive living/dining area and island kitchen. A multitude of windows fills the interior with sunlight and ocean breezes. The wraparound rear deck finds access near the kitchen. The utility room is conveniently tucked between the kitchen and the two first-floor bedrooms. The second-floor master suite offers a private deck and a luxurious bath with a garden tub, shower, and walk-in closet.

Balcony 14'x 7'

Master Bedroom 21'x 18'

Open To Below

WIC

Ma. Bath

SECOND FLOOR

Wood Deck 24'8"x 12'

Porch 14'x 7'

Kitchen 14'x 14'

Util.

Bedroom 13'4"x 14'

Living/Dining 16'x 25'6"

WIC

Foyer

Bath

Porch 21'6"x 8'

Bedroom 13'4"x 11'4"

FIRST FLOOR

HIGH TIDE
BEST-SELLING WATERFRONT HOMES IN FULL COLOR

plan # HPK0200005

STYLE: COLONIAL
FIRST FLOOR: 2,200 SQ. FT.
SECOND FLOOR: 1,001 SQ. FT.
TOTAL: 3,201 SQ. FT.
BONUS SPACE: 674 SQ. FT.
BEDROOMS: 4
BATHROOMS: 3½
WIDTH: 70' - 4"
DEPTH: 74' - 4"
FOUNDATION: CRAWLSPACE

SEARCH ONLINE @ EPLANS.COM

A wide, welcoming front porch and three dormer windows lend Southern flair to this charming farmhouse. Inside, three fireplaces—found in the living, dining, and family rooms—create a cozy atmosphere. The family room opens to the covered rear porch, and the breakfast area opens to a small side porch. Sleeping quarters include a luxurious first-floor master suite—with a private bath and two walk-in closets—as well as three family bedrooms upstairs.

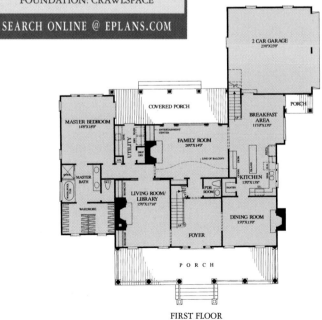

FIRST FLOOR

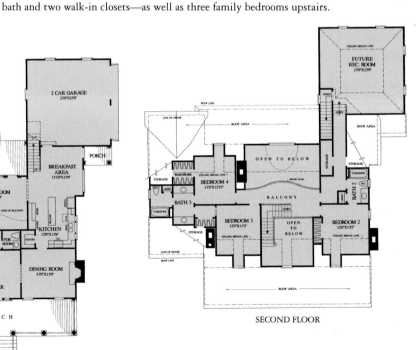

SECOND FLOOR

HIGH TIDE
BEST-SELLING WATERFRONT HOMES IN FULL COLOR

plan# HPK0200006

STYLE: COLONIAL
SQUARE FOOTAGE: 2,595
BONUS SPACE: 1,480 SQ. FT.
BEDROOMS: 4
BATHROOMS: 2½
WIDTH: 78' - 8"
DEPTH: 67' - 0"
FOUNDATION: BASEMENT

SEARCH ONLINE @ EPLANS.COM

This home has a touch of modernism with all the comforts of country style. The pillared front porch allows for summer evening relaxation. The foyer extends into the bright great room equipped with a fireplace. The large kitchen is stationed between the vaulted dining room and airy breakfast nook. Two walk-in closets, dual vanities, and a spacious bath complement the master suite. Each of the three family bedrooms features closet space. The entire second floor is left for future development, whether it be a guest room, rec room, study, or all three.

Future
9-3x6-4

Future
12-6x18-0

Future
24-0x11-10

Future
36-0x18-0

Future
23-6x8-2

M.Bath
19-0x11-3

Master
Bedroom
19-0x14-0

Porch
17-4x6-6

Breakfast
13-0x11-6

Laundry
9-4x5-6

Storage
13-0x5-6

½ Bath

Bedroom
14-0x12-0

Bath

Greatroom
16-10x20-0

Kitchen
14-6x13-0

Garage
22-8x27-3

Bedroom
12-10x12-8

Bedroom
13-0x12-2

Foyer
8-0x16-0

Dining
13-0x14-0

Porch
24-8x7-4

HIGH TIDE
BEST-SELLING WATERFRONT HOMES IN FULL COLOR

plan# HPK0200007

STYLE: FARMHOUSE
FIRST FLOOR: 2,648 SQ. FT.
SECOND FLOOR: 1,253 SQ. FT.
TOTAL: 3,901 SQ. FT.
BONUS SPACE: 540 SQ. FT.
BEDROOMS: 4
BATHROOMS: 3½
WIDTH: 82' - 0"
DEPTH: 60' - 4"
FOUNDATION: CRAWLSPACE

SEARCH ONLINE @ EPLANS.COM

This delightful home packs quite a punch. The grand staircase in the elegant foyer makes a dazzling first impression. To the left is the living room and on the right is the library, which opens to the sunroom overlooking the deck. The angled, island kitchen is situated conveniently between the breakfast area and the dining room. The master suite finds privacy on the far right. Here the private bath pampers with spaceousness and twin wardrobes. Four additional bedrooms are found on the second floor along with three full baths.

SECOND FLOOR

FIRST FLOOR

HIGH TIDE
BEST-SELLING WATERFRONT HOMES IN FULL COLOR

French style embellishes this dormered country home. Stepping through French doors to the foyer, the dining area is immediately to the left. To the right is a set of double doors leading to a study or secondary bedroom. A lavish master bedroom provides privacy and plenty of storage space. The living room sports three doors to the rear porch and a lovely fireplace with built-ins. A secluded breakfast nook adjoins an efficient kitchen. Upstairs, two of the three family bedrooms boast dormer windows. Plans include a basement-level garage that adjoins a game room and two handy storage areas.

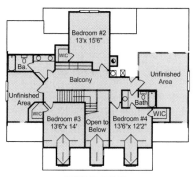

plan# HPK0200008

STYLE: COUNTRY COTTAGE
FIRST FLOOR: 2,129 SQ. FT.
SECOND FLOOR: 1,206 SQ. FT.
TOTAL: 3,335 SQ. FT.
BONUS SPACE: 422 SQ. FT.
BEDROOMS: 4
BATHROOMS: 4
WIDTH: 59' - 4"
DEPTH: 64' - 0"
FOUNDATION: BASEMENT
FINISHED BASEMENT: 435 SQ. FT.

SEARCH ONLINE @ EPLANS.COM

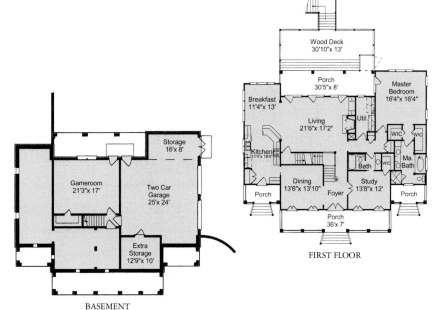

BASEMENT

FIRST FLOOR

SECOND FLOOR

HIGH TIDE

BEST-SELLING WATERFRONT HOMES IN FULL COLOR

plan# HPK0200009

STYLE: COUNTRY COTTAGE
FIRST FLOOR: 2,036 SQ. FT.
SECOND FLOOR: 1,230 SQ. FT.
TOTAL: 3,266 SQ. FT.
BEDROOMS: 5
BATHROOMS: 3½
WIDTH: 57' - 4"
DEPTH: 59' - 0"
FOUNDATION: PIER

SEARCH ONLINE @ EPLANS.COM

The standing-seam metal roof adds character to this four- (or five-) bedroom home. The covered front porch, screened porch, and rear deck add outdoor living spaces for nature enthusiasts. A flexible room is found to the left of the foyer, while the dining room is to the right. The galley kitchen is accessed through an archway with a sunny breakfast nook adjoining at the back. The lavish master suite is on the left with a private bath that includes access to the laundry room. The second floor holds three bedrooms and a multimedia room where the family can spend quality time in a casual atmosphere.

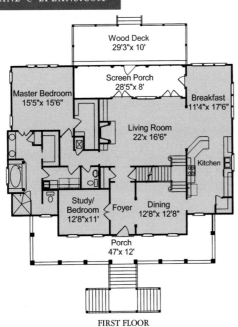

FIRST FLOOR

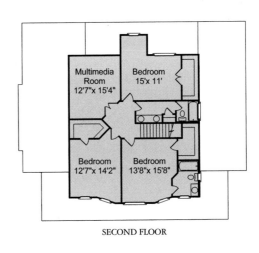

SECOND FLOOR

HIGH TIDE
BEST-SELLING WATERFRONT HOMES IN FULL COLOR

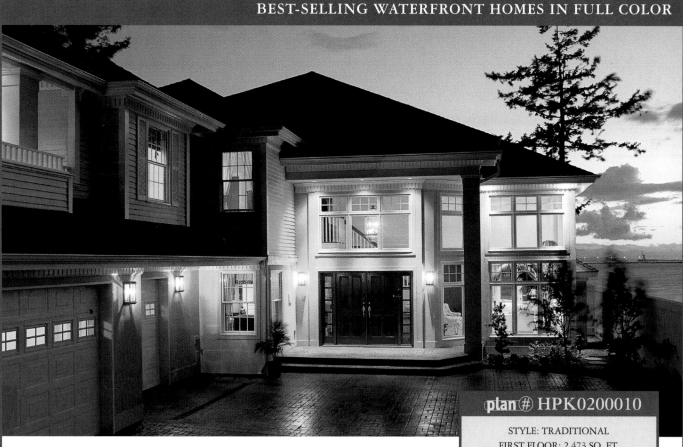

This unusual stucco-and-siding design opens with a grand portico to a foyer that extends to the living room with a fireplace. Proceed up a few steps to the dining room with its coffered ceiling and butler's pantry, which connects to the gourmet kitchen. The attached hearth room has the requisite fireplace and three sets of French doors to the covered porch. The family room sports a coffered ceiling and a fireplace flanked by French doors. The second floor boasts four bedrooms, including a master suite with a tray ceiling, covered deck, and lavish bath. Two full baths serve the family bedrooms and a bonus room that might be used as an additional bedroom or hobby space.

plan # HPK0200010

STYLE: TRADITIONAL
FIRST FLOOR: 2,473 SQ. FT.
SECOND FLOOR: 2,686 SQ. FT.
TOTAL: 5,159 SQ. FT.
BONUS SPACE: 337 SQ. FT.
BEDROOMS: 4
BATHROOMS: 4½
WIDTH: 57' - 8"
DEPTH: 103' - 6"
FOUNDATION: BASEMENT

SEARCH ONLINE @ EPLANS.COM

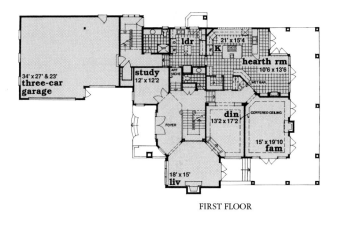

FIRST FLOOR

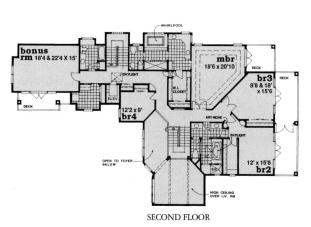

SECOND FLOOR

HIGH TIDE
BEST-SELLING WATERFRONT HOMES IN FULL COLOR

plan # HPK0200011

STYLE: TRANSITIONAL
FIRST FLOOR: 2,577 SQ. FT.
SECOND FLOOR: 1,703 SQ. FT.
TOTAL: 4,280 SQ. FT.
BEDROOMS: 4
BATHROOMS: 3½
WIDTH: 80' - 4"
DEPTH: 85' - 11"
FOUNDATION: CRAWLSPACE

SEARCH ONLINE @ EPLANS.COM

Arched windows, soaring ceilings, and bright spaces make this resort-style home a dream come true. A grand entry opens to the formal foyer; to the left, the hearth-warmed study is both comfortable and dignified; ahead, the two-story great room encourages gatherings around the fireplace and expands out to the terrace through French doors. The dining room (with a wet bar), breakfast nook, and sunroom are effortlessly served by the cooktop-island kitchen. The vaulted master suite enjoys abundant natural light and a luxurious spa bath. Upstairs, secondary suites are anything but inferior, with private or semiprivate baths, generous dimensions, and access to a sunken sitting room and a recreation room with a veranda.

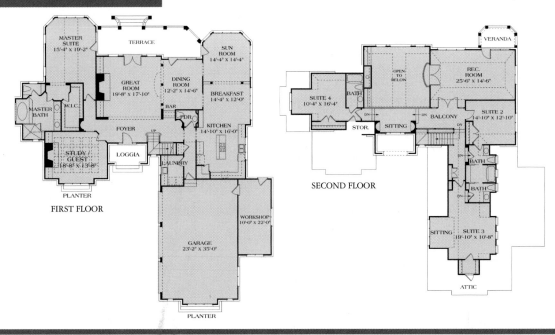

FIRST FLOOR

SECOND FLOOR

HIGH TIDE
BEST-SELLING WATERFRONT HOMES IN FULL COLOR

Special details make the difference between a house and a home. A snack bar, an audiovisual center, and a fireplace make the family room a favorite place for informal gatherings. A desk, an island cooktop, a bay, and skylights enhance the kitchen area. The dining room features two columns and a plant ledge. The first-floor master suite includes His and Hers walk-in closets, a spacious bath, and a bay window. On the second floor, one bedroom features a walk-in closet and private bath; two additional bedrooms share a full bath.

plan# HPK0200012

STYLE: SW CONTEMPORARY
FIRST FLOOR: 2,022 SQ. FT.
SECOND FLOOR: 845 SQ. FT.
TOTAL: 2,867 SQ. FT.
BEDROOMS: 5
BATHROOMS: 4
WIDTH: 63' - 8"
DEPTH: 56' - 2"
FOUNDATION: SLAB

SEARCH ONLINE @ EPLANS.COM

FIRST FLOOR

SECOND FLOOR

HIGH TIDE
BEST-SELLING WATERFRONT HOMES IN FULL COLOR

PHOTO BY: KIM SARGENT

THIS HOME, AS SHOWN IN THE PHOTOGRAPH, MAY DIFFER FROM THE ACTUAL BLUEPRINTS. FOR MORE DETAILED INFORMATION, PLEASE CHECK THE FLOOR PLANS CARFFULLY

plan# HPK0200013

STYLE: FRENCH
SQUARE FOOTAGE: 3,723
BONUS SPACE: 390 SQ. FT.
BEDROOMS: 5
BATHROOMS: 4
WIDTH: 82' - 4"
DEPTH: 89' - 0"
FOUNDATION: SLAB

SEARCH ONLINE @ EPLANS.COM

The warmth of brick facade treatments, intricate molding detailing, and classic Palladian windows set this home apart from the rest. The wood detailing continues inside this magnificent home. The floor plan is a play on octagonal shapes, which create angular vistas throughout the home. Columns and pediments greet you in the formal living and dining rooms, bathed in natural light. The master suite enjoys all the latest amenities, including a sitting room, trayed ceilings, His and Hers bath appointments, doorless shower, and huge closets. The family side of this home enjoys tile-lined traffic areas, large bedrooms, an island kitchen, and a bonus room, which can overlook the golf course or lake, with balcony. Details like a window in the laundry room and direct access to the three car garage, make this the perfect house.

REAR EXTERIOR

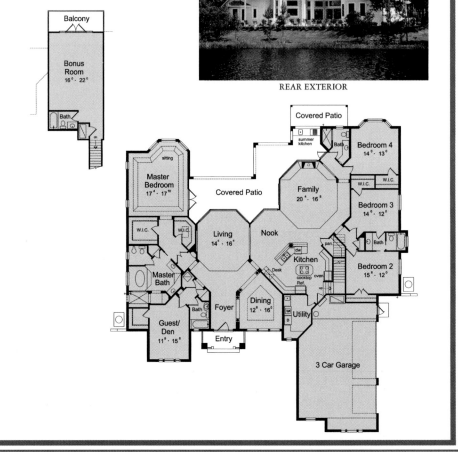

HIGH TIDE
BEST-SELLING WATERFRONT HOMES IN FULL COLOR

plan# HPK0200014

STYLE: COLONIAL
FIRST FLOOR: 2,144 SQ. FT.
SECOND FLOOR: 1,253 SQ. FT.
TOTAL: 3,397 SQ. FT.
BEDROOMS: 3
BATHROOMS: 3½
WIDTH: 64' - 11"
DEPTH: 76' - 7"

SEARCH ONLINE @ EPLANS.COM

This two-story beauty is rich in luxurious style. A dramatic entrance welcomes you to the foyer, where a stunning curved staircase greets you. A turret-style dining room is flooded with light from the bayed windows. Across the gallery, the living room features a through-fireplace to the family room. The island kitchen is open to the breakfast room, which accesses the rear porch and the family room equipped with built-ins. The first-floor master bedroom offers a bath with a whirlpool tub, two walk-in closets, and a dressing room. Two additional bedrooms, a study, and a game room with sundeck access all reside on the second floor.

FIRST FLOOR

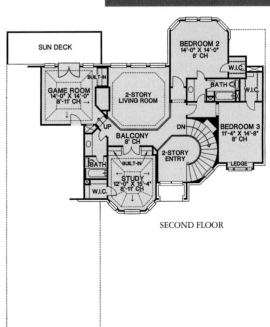

SECOND FLOOR

HIGH TIDE
BEST-SELLING WATERFRONT HOMES IN FULL COLOR

plan# HPK0200015

STYLE: TRADITIONAL
FIRST FLOOR: 1,715 SQ. FT.
SECOND FLOOR: 620 SQ. FT.
TOTAL: 2,335 SQ. FT.
BONUS SPACE: 265 SQ. FT.
BEDROOMS: 3
BATHROOMS: 2½
WIDTH: 58' - 6"
DEPTH: 50' - 3"

SEARCH ONLINE @ EPLANS.COM

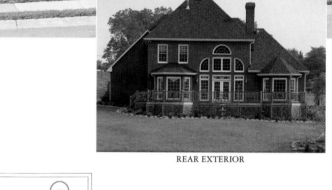

REAR EXTERIOR

With a delightful flavor, this two-story home features family living at its best. The foyer opens to a study or living room on the left. The dining room on the right offers large proportions and full windows. The family room remains open to the kitchen and the breakfast room. Here, sunny meals are guaranteed with a bay window overlooking the rear yard. In the master suite, a bayed sitting area, a walk-in closet, and a pampering bath are sure to please. Upstairs, two family bedrooms flank a loft or study area.

FIRST FLOOR

PATIO

spa

sitting

MASTER BED RM.
14-0 x 13-9

FAMILY RM.
17-8 x 20-0
(two story)

BRKFST.
9-6 x 8-7

KIT.
13-11 x 8-10

fireplace

walk-in closet

balcony above

pd. rm.

cl

UTIL.
7-3 x 7-10

storage

master bath

up

pantry

cl

FOYER
7-0 x 9-10

DINING RM.
12-4 x 13-0

GARAGE
21-2 x 21-8

STUDY/ LIVING
12-0 x 11-0

fireplace

© 1994 Donald A. Gardner Architects, Inc.

SECOND FLOOR

clerestory window with arched top

BED RM.
13-7 x 11-0

great room below

walk-in closet

LOFT/ STUDY
8-4 x 12-5

railing

bath

attic storage

down

attic storage

walk-in closet

foyer below

BED RM.
12-4 x 13-0

lin.

skylights

BONUS RM.
11-4 x 21-8

HIGH TIDE
BEST-SELLING WATERFRONT HOMES IN FULL COLOR

plan# HPK0200016

STYLE: TRADITIONAL
FIRST FLOOR: 2,167 SQ. FT.
SECOND FLOOR: 891 SQ. FT.
TOTAL: 3,058 SQ. FT.
BONUS SPACE: 252 SQ. FT.
BEDROOMS: 4
BATHROOMS: 3
WIDTH: 64' - 5"
DEPTH: 74' - 0"
FOUNDATION: CRAWLSPACE

SEARCH ONLINE @ EPLANS.COM

This traditional home contains elements of country style and a relaxed attitude that make it great for the waterfront or the suburbs. An inviting portico entry opens to the foyer, which leads ahead to the sun-drenched great room. A central staircase separate the great room from the gourmet kitchen that easily serves the dining room and sunny breakfast nook. A rear deck/terrace is accessible from this area. To the left, a den or guest suite has a semiprivate bath. The master suite claims the right wing, indulging in a magnificent bath and filled with natural light. Two bedrooms located upstairs share a full bath and access to a bonus room and recreation loft. A balcony overlook leads to convenient walk-in storage.

FIRST FLOOR

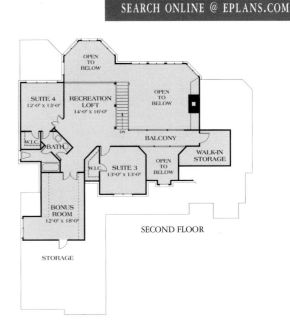

SECOND FLOOR

HIGH TIDE
BEST-SELLING WATERFRONT HOMES IN FULL COLOR

plan# HPK0200017

STYLE: COUNTRY COTTAGE
FIRST FLOOR: 1,804 SQ. FT.
SECOND FLOOR: 1,041 SQ. FT.
TOTAL: 2,845 SQ. FT.
BEDROOMS: 4
BATHROOMS: 3½
WIDTH: 57' - 3"
DEPTH: 71' - 0"
FOUNDATION: WALKOUT BASEMENT

SEARCH ONLINE @ EPLANS.COM

There's a feeling of old Charleston in this stately home—particularly on the quiet side porch that wraps around the kitchen and breakfast room. The interior of this home revolves around a spacious great room with a welcoming fireplace. The left wing is dedicated to the master suite, which boasts wide views of the rear property. A corner kitchen easily serves planned events in the formal dining room, as well as family meals in the breakfast area. Three family bedrooms, one with a private bath and the others sharing a bath, are tucked upstairs.

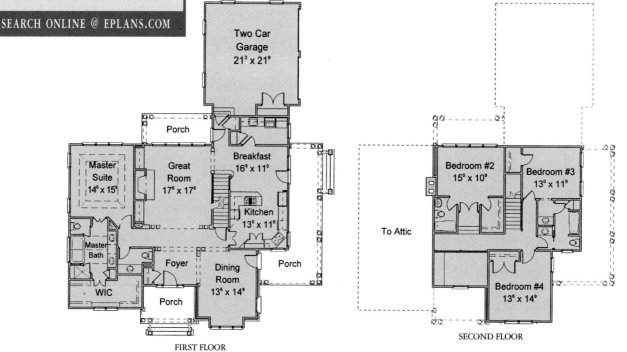

FIRST FLOOR

SECOND FLOOR

REAR EXTERIOR

plan# HPK0200018

STYLE: FARMHOUSE
FIRST FLOOR: 2,628 SQ. FT.
SECOND FLOOR: 1,775 SQ. FT.
TOTAL: 4,403 SQ. FT.
BEDROOMS: 5
BATHROOMS: 3½
WIDTH: 79' - 6"
DEPTH: 65' - 1"
FOUNDATION: WALKOUT BASEMENT

SEARCH ONLINE @ EPLANS.COM

With five bedrooms and a wonderful stone-and-siding exterior, this country home will satisfy every need. Two sets of French doors provide access to the dining room and foyer. The great room enjoys a warming fireplace and deck access. The kitchen, breakfast bay, and keeping room feature an open floor plan. A charming sitting area in a bay window sets off the master bedroom. The master bath features a large walk-in closet, two-sink vanity, separate tub and shower, and compartmented toilet. Four bedrooms, an office, and two full baths complete the upper level.

SECOND FLOOR

Office 12³x19⁹
Open to below
Bedroom #5 15⁵x14⁶
Bedroom #2 19³x20⁰
Bedroom #3 13⁶x16⁰
Bedroom #4 11³x13

FIRST FLOOR

Breakfast 15⁵x13⁹
Deck
Master Bedroom 15⁵x14⁶
One Car Garage 13x22
Keeping Room 15⁵x17⁹
Kitchen 15⁵x14⁵
Great Room 18⁶x19⁶
Master Bath
Dining Room 13⁰x15⁶
Two Car Garage 23³x24
Foyer
Porch

HIGH TIDE
BEST-SELLING WATERFRONT HOMES IN FULL COLOR

plan# HPK0200019

STYLE: CRAFTSMAN
FIRST FLOOR: 2,665 SQ. FT.
SECOND FLOOR: 1,081 SQ. FT.
TOTAL: 3,746 SQ. FT.
BEDROOMS: 4
BATHROOMS: 3½
WIDTH: 88' - 0"
DEPTH: 52' - 6"
FOUNDATION: BASEMENT

SEARCH ONLINE @ EPLANS.COM

This lovely plan steps into the future with an exterior mix of brick, stone, and cedar siding. With a large front porch, the home appears as if it should be located in a quaint oceanfront community. Comfortable elegance coupled with modern-day amenities and nostalgic materials makes this home a great choice. The large great room and hearth room/breakfast area offer grand views to the rear yard, where a large deck complements outdoor activities.

SECOND FLOOR

FIRST FLOOR

ORDER BLUEPRINTS 24 HOURS, 7 DAYS A WEEK, AT 1-800-521-6797

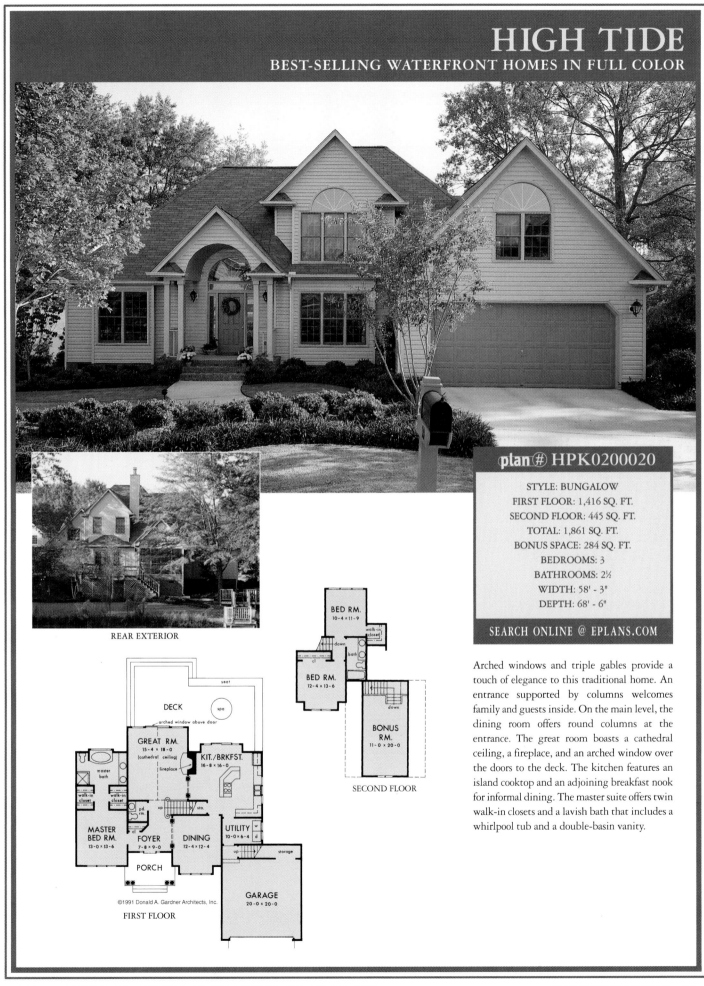

HIGH TIDE
BEST-SELLING WATERFRONT HOMES IN FULL COLOR

REAR EXTERIOR

plan# HPK0200020

STYLE: BUNGALOW
FIRST FLOOR: 1,416 SQ. FT.
SECOND FLOOR: 445 SQ. FT.
TOTAL: 1,861 SQ. FT.
BONUS SPACE: 284 SQ. FT.
BEDROOMS: 3
BATHROOMS: 2½
WIDTH: 58' - 3"
DEPTH: 68' - 6"

SEARCH ONLINE @ EPLANS.COM

Arched windows and triple gables provide a touch of elegance to this traditional home. An entrance supported by columns welcomes family and guests inside. On the main level, the dining room offers round columns at the entrance. The great room boasts a cathedral ceiling, a fireplace, and an arched window over the doors to the deck. The kitchen features an island cooktop and an adjoining breakfast nook for informal dining. The master suite offers twin walk-in closets and a lavish bath that includes a whirlpool tub and a double-basin vanity.

SECOND FLOOR

BED RM.
10-4 × 11-9

BED RM.
12-4 × 13-6

BONUS RM.
11-0 × 20-0

DECK

spa

GREAT RM.
15-4 × 18-0
(cathedral ceiling)
fireplace

KIT./BRKFST.
16-8 × 16-0

master bath

walk-in closet

walk-in closet

MASTER BED RM.
13-0 × 13-6

FOYER
7-8 × 9-0

DINING
12-4 × 12-4

UTILITY
10-0 × 6-4

PORCH

GARAGE
20-0 × 20-0

storage

©1991 Donald A. Gardner Architects, Inc.

FIRST FLOOR

HIGH TIDE
BEST-SELLING WATERFRONT HOMES IN FULL COLOR

ANDREW LAUTMAN, LAUTMAN PHOTOGRAPHY

THIS HOME, AS SHOWN IN THE PHOTOGRAPH, MAY DIFFER FROM THE ACTUAL BLUEPRINTS. FOR MORE DETAILED INFORMATION, PLEASE CHECK THE FLOOR PLANS CAREFULLY.

REAR EXTERIOR

plan# HPK0200021

STYLE: CAPE COD
FIRST FLOOR: 1,387 SQ. FT.
SECOND FLOOR: 929 SQ. FT.
TOTAL: 2,316 SQ. FT.
BEDROOMS: 4
BATHROOMS: 3
WIDTH: 30' - 0"
DEPTH: 51' - 8"
FOUNDATION: CRAWLSPACE

SEARCH ONLINE @ EPLANS.COM

Perfect for a narrow lot, this shingle-and-stone Nantucket Cape home caters to the casual lifestyle. The side entrance gives direct access to the wonderfully open living areas: gathering room with fireplace and an abundance of windows; island kitchen with angled, pass-through snack bar; and dining area with sliding glass doors to a covered eating area. Note also the large deck that further extends the living potential. Also on this floor is the large master suite with a compartmented bath, private dressing room, and walk-in closet. Upstairs, you'll find the three family bedrooms. Of the two bedrooms that share a bath, one features a private balcony.

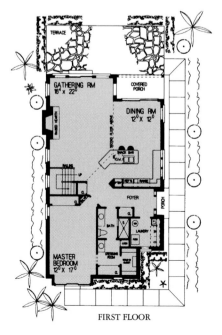

FIRST FLOOR

SECOND FLOOR

ORDER BLUEPRINTS 24 HOURS, 7 DAYS A WEEK, AT 1-800-521-6797

HIGH TIDE
BEST-SELLING WATERFRONT HOMES IN FULL COLOR

This traditional design is accented in Craftsman architecture and features two lavish levels of livability for the whole family. Inside, a formal dining room and library flank the foyer. The two-story great room is warmed by an enormous fireplace flanked by built-ins. Casual areas of the home include the island kitchen, breakfast nook, and bay-windowed hearth room. The first-floor master suite offers two walk-in closets and a lavish private bath enjoying a whirlpool tub. A three-car garage and laundry room complete the first floor. Three additional bedrooms and two baths are located upstairs.

plan# HPK0200022

STYLE: CRAFTSMAN
FIRST FLOOR: 2,702 SQ. FT.
SECOND FLOOR: 986 SQ. FT.
TOTAL: 3,688 SQ. FT.
BEDROOMS: 4
BATHROOMS: 3½
WIDTH: 75' - 0"
DEPTH: 64' - 11"
FOUNDATION: BASEMENT

SEARCH ONLINE @ EPLANS.COM

FIRST FLOOR

SECOND FLOOR

HIGH TIDE
BEST-SELLING WATERFRONT HOMES IN FULL COLOR

plan # HPK0200023

STYLE: FARMHOUSE
FIRST FLOOR: 2,837 SQ. FT.
SECOND FLOOR: 609 SQ. FT.
TOTAL: 3,446 SQ. FT.
BEDROOMS: 4
BATHROOMS: 4
WIDTH: 68' - 0"
DEPTH: 83' - 4"
FOUNDATION: SLAB

SEARCH ONLINE @ EPLANS.COM

Gable-on-gable details and an entry adorned with thick columns creates a distinctly interesting exterior for this four-bedroom home. The den and formal dining rooms take their traditional position near the entry for this design. At the center of the plan, the family room enjoys a warming fireplace. To the left are two family bedrooms and a den/study and to the right are the gourmet kitchen and breakfast nook. The luxurious master suite contains many amenities, including a tray ceiling, a walk-in closet, French-door access to the rear patio, and a sumptuous bathroom with a corner oval soaking tub. Bedroom 4 features a full bath and a sitting room on the second floor.

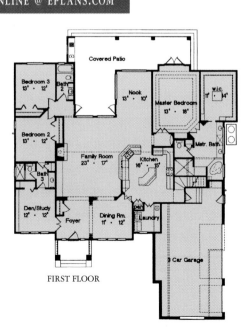

FIRST FLOOR

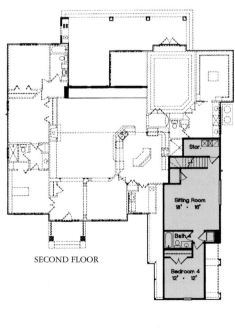

SECOND FLOOR

HIGH TIDE
BEST-SELLING WATERFRONT HOMES IN FULL COLOR

This Early American design offers great livability with an expansive living room accented by a fireplace. Nearby, an efficient island kitchen serves the formal dining room and a cozy breakfast nook. A quiet study with built-in bookshelves sits to the left of the foyer. Upstairs, the master bedroom includes a walk-in closet and a private bath; two family bedrooms share a full dual-vanity bath just across the hall.

plan# HPK0200024

STYLE: EUROPEAN COTTAGE
FIRST FLOOR: 1,388 SQ. FT.
SECOND FLOOR: 809 SQ. FT.
TOTAL: 2,197 SQ. FT.
BEDROOMS: 3
BATHROOMS: 2½
WIDTH: 73' - 4"
DEPTH: 32' - 0"
FOUNDATION: BASEMENT

SEARCH ONLINE @ EPLANS.COM

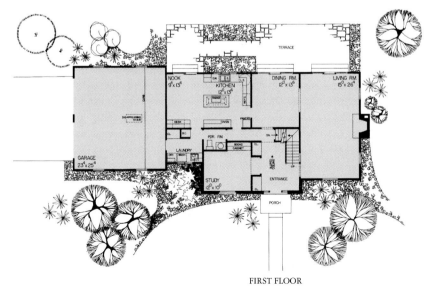

FIRST FLOOR

SECOND FLOOR

HIGH TIDE
BEST-SELLING WATERFRONT HOMES IN FULL COLOR

plan# HPK0200025

STYLE: VACATION
FIRST FLOOR: 1,235 SQ. FT.
SECOND FLOOR: 543 SQ. FT.
TOTAL: 1,778 SQ. FT.
BEDROOMS: 3
BATHROOMS: 2
WIDTH: 27' - 6"
DEPTH: 46' - 0"
FOUNDATION: CRAWLSPACE, BASEMENT

SEARCH ONLINE @ EPLANS.COM

An expansive sundeck with an optional spa wraps around this design to highlight outdoor living. Tall windows accent the vaulted ceiling in the living and dining rooms. Both areas are warmed by a central fireplace flanked by doors to the deck. A U-shaped kitchen is open to the dining room. Two bedrooms with walk-in closets sit to the back of the first floor and share the use of a full bath. The master suite dominates the upper level and has a full bath and large wall closet. Note the laundry room and service entrance on the first floor.

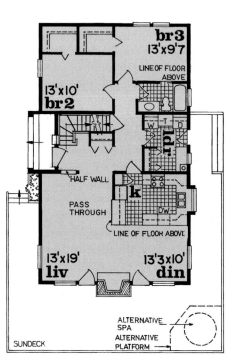

FIRST FLOOR

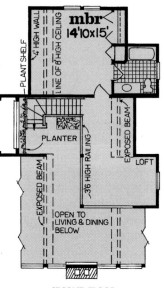

SECOND FLOOR

RISE TO THE OCCASION
HILLSIDE LIVING AND ELEVATED FOUNDATIONS

FIRST FLOOR

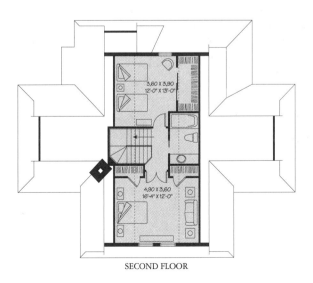

SECOND FLOOR

plan # HPK0200026

STYLE: LAKEFRONT
FIRST FLOOR: 1,212 SQ. FT.
SECOND FLOOR: 620 SQ. FT.
TOTAL: 1,832 SQ. FT.
BEDROOMS: 3
BATHROOMS: 2
WIDTH: 38' - 0"
DEPTH: 40' - 0"
FOUNDATION: BASEMENT

SEARCH ONLINE @ EPLANS.COM

This comfortable vacation design provides two levels of relaxing family space. The main level offers a spacious wrapping front porch and an abundance of windows, filling interior spaces with the summer sunshine. A two-sided fireplace warms the living room/dining room combination and a master bedroom that features a roomy walk-in closet. Nearby, the hall bath offers a relaxing whirlpool tub. The kitchen is open and features an island snack bar and pantry storage. A cozy sunroom accesses the wrapping deck. Upstairs, two additional bedrooms feature ample closet space and share a second-floor bath.

RISE TO THE OCCASION
HILLSIDE LIVING AND ELEVATED FOUNDATIONS

plan # HPK0200027

STYLE: MOUNTAIN
FIRST FLOOR: 856 SQ. FT.
SECOND FLOOR: 636 SQ. FT.
TOTAL: 1,492 SQ. FT.
BEDROOMS: 3
BATHROOMS: 1½
WIDTH: 44' - 0"
DEPTH: 26' - 0"
FOUNDATION: BASEMENT

SEARCH ONLINE @ EPLANS.COM

A standing-seam metal roof, horizontal siding, and a massive deck combine to create a mosaic of parallel lines on this rustic two-story home. Sunlight spills into the great room through four beautiful clerestory windows. A generous L-shaped kitchen with a work island adjoins the dining area. A bedroom and powder room are neatly tucked behind the staircase that leads to the second-floor sleeping quarters. Upstairs, a loft allows plenty of space for a computer in kick-off-your-shoes comfort.

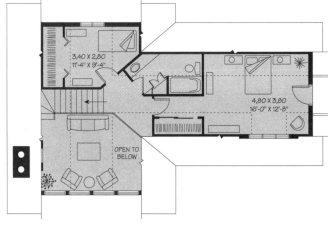

SECOND FLOOR

FIRST FLOOR

RISE TO THE OCCASION
HILLSIDE LIVING AND ELEVATED FOUNDATIONS

plan# HPK0200028

STYLE: SEASIDE
FIRST FLOOR: 962 SQ. FT.
SECOND FLOOR: 1,076 SQ. FT.
THIRD FLOOR: 342 SQ. FT.
TOTAL: 2,380 SQ. FT.
BEDROOMS: 5
BATHROOMS: 3½
WIDTH: 39' - 8"
DEPTH: 36' - 8"
FOUNDATION: PIER

SEARCH ONLINE @ EPLANS.COM

This three-level beach house offers spectacular views all around. With three deck levels accessible from all living areas, the outside sea air will surround you. The first level enjoys a living room, three bedrooms, a full bath, and a laundry area. The second level expands to a family area, a dining room, and a kitchen with an island snack bar and nearby half-bath. The master suite enjoys a walk-through closet and an amenity-filled bath with dual vanities and a separate tub and shower. The third level is a private haven—perfect for another bedroom—complete with a bath, walk-in closet, and sitting area.

FIRST FLOOR

SECOND FLOOR

THIRD FLOOR

RISE TO THE OCCASION
HILLSIDE LIVING AND ELEVATED FOUNDATIONS

plan# HPK0200029

STYLE: LAKEFRONT
FIRST FLOOR: 895 SQ. FT.
SECOND FLOOR: 565 SQ. FT.
TOTAL: 1,460 SQ. FT.
BEDROOMS: 2
BATHROOMS: 1½
WIDTH: 38' - 0"
DEPTH: 36' - 0"
FOUNDATION: BASEMENT

SEARCH ONLINE @ EPLANS.COM

This four-season Cape Cod cottage is perfect for a site with great views. A sunroom provides wide vistas and easy indoor/outdoor flow. The living area boasts a corner fireplace. A well-organized kitchen serves a snack counter as well as the dining room. A laundry room and petite rear storage area round out this floor. Upstairs, two spacious bedrooms share a lavish bath, which is complete with a window tub and separate shower.

SECOND FLOOR

FIRST FLOOR

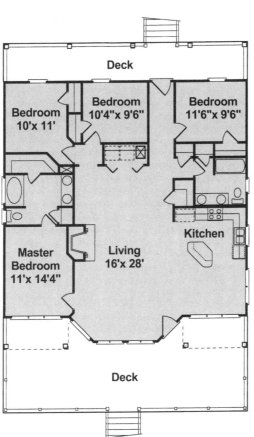

plan# HPK0200030

STYLE: VACATION
SQUARE FOOTAGE: 1,520
BEDROOMS: 4
BATHROOMS: 2
WIDTH: 40' - 0"
DEPTH: 59' - 0"
FOUNDATION: CRAWLSPACE, PIER

SEARCH ONLINE @ EPLANS.COM

Size doesn't always predict amenities! This one-story pier-foundation home is only 1,520 square feet, but it's packed with surprises. The spacious living room offers a huge wall of windows to show off the beach, and a fireplace offers warmth on cool winter evenings. The L-shaped kitchen features an angled work island and easily accesses the adjacent dining area. Three secondary bedrooms share a full bath and provide ample room for family or guests. The master bedroom is complete with a walk-in closet and a private bath.

RISE TO THE OCCASION
HILLSIDE LIVING AND ELEVATED FOUNDATIONS

plan # HPK0200031

STYLE: SEASIDE
FIRST FLOOR: 1,056 SQ. FT.
SECOND FLOOR: 807 SQ. FT.
TOTAL: 1,863 SQ. FT.
BEDROOMS: 4
BATHROOMS: 3
WIDTH: 33' - 0"
DEPTH: 54' - 0"
FOUNDATION: CRAWLSPACE, PIER

SEARCH ONLINE @ EPLANS.COM

Run up a flight of stairs to an attractive four-bedroom home! The living room features a fireplace and easy access to the L-shaped kitchen. Here, a work island makes meal preparation a breeze. Two family bedrooms share a full bath and access to the laundry facilities. Upstairs, a third bedroom offers a private bath and two walk-in closets. The master suite is complete with a pampering bath, two walk-in closets, and a large private balcony.

SECOND FLOOR

FIRST FLOOR

RISE TO THE OCCASION
HILLSIDE LIVING AND ELEVATED FOUNDATIONS

With a pier foundation, this two-story home is perfect for an oceanfront lot. The main level consists of an open living area that flows into the dining area adjacent to the kitchen. Here, a walk-in pantry and plenty of counter and cabinet space will please the gourmet of the family. A full bath and a utility room complete this floor. Upstairs, the sleeping zone is complete with two family bedrooms sharing a linen closet and a full hall bath, as well as a deluxe master bedroom. Features here include a private balcony, a walk-in closet, and a dual-vanity bath.

plan # HPK0200032

STYLE: SEASIDE
FIRST FLOOR: 912 SQ. FT.
SECOND FLOOR: 831 SQ. FT.
TOTAL: 1,743 SQ. FT.
BEDROOMS: 3
BATHROOMS: 3
WIDTH: 34' - 0"
DEPTH: 32' - 0"
FOUNDATION: PIER

SEARCH ONLINE @ EPLANS.COM

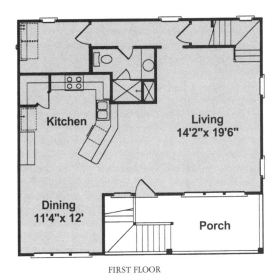

Kitchen

Living
14'2"x 19'6"

Dining
11'4"x 12'

Porch

FIRST FLOOR

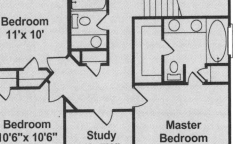

Bedroom
11'x 10'

Bedroom
10'6"x 10'6"

Study
9'x 7'3"

Master Bedroom
13'x 14'

Balcony

SECOND FLOOR

RISE TO THE OCCASION
HILLSIDE LIVING AND ELEVATED FOUNDATIONS

plan # HPK0200033

STYLE: TIDEWATER

FIRST FLOOR: 2,096 SQ. FT.

SECOND FLOOR: 892 SQ. FT.

TOTAL: 2,988 SQ. FT.

BEDROOMS: 3

BATHROOMS: 3½

WIDTH: 58' - 0"

DEPTH: 54' - 0"

FOUNDATION: ISLAND BASEMENT

SEARCH ONLINE @ EPLANS.COM

The variety in the rooflines of this striking waterfront home will certainly make it the envy of the neighborhood. The two-story great room, with its fireplace and built-ins, is a short flight down from the foyer. The three sets of French doors give access to the covered lanai. The huge well-equipped kitchen will easily serve the gourmet who loves to entertain. The stepped ceiling and bay window in the dining room will add style to every meal. The master suite completes the first level. Two bedrooms and two full baths, along with an expansive loft, constitute the second level. Bedroom 3 has an attached sundeck.

SECOND FLOOR

FIRST FLOOR

BASEMENT

ORDER BLUEPRINTS 24 HOURS, 7 DAYS A WEEK, AT 1-800-521-6797

The staircase leading to a columned front porch lends a touch of grandeur to this residence. The great room is made inviting with a fireplace and twin sets of double doors opening to a wraparound porch that's also accessed by the master suite. This spacious suite features luxurious extras like His and Hers sinks, a separate garden tub and shower, and a huge walk-in closet. The kitchen provides plenty of counter space and overlooks the formal dining room. Upstairs, two additional bedrooms open up to a second-floor porch and have their own private baths and walk-in closets.

plan# HPK0200034

STYLE: SEASIDE
FIRST FLOOR: 1,492 SQ. FT.
SECOND FLOOR: 854 SQ. FT.
TOTAL: 2,346 SQ. FT.
BEDROOMS: 3
BATHROOMS: 3½
WIDTH: 44' - 0"
DEPTH: 48' - 0"
FOUNDATION: ISLAND BASEMENT

SEARCH ONLINE @ EPLANS.COM

BASEMENT

FIRST FLOOR

SECOND FLOOR

RISE TO THE OCCASION
HILLSIDE LIVING AND ELEVATED FOUNDATIONS

plan# HPK0200035

STYLE: FLORIDIAN
FIRST FLOOR: 1,586 SQ. FT.
SECOND FLOOR: 601 SQ. FT.
TOTAL: 2,187 SQ. FT.
BEDROOMS: 3
BATHROOMS: 2
WIDTH: 50' - 0"
DEPTH: 44' - 0"
FOUNDATION: PIER

SEARCH ONLINE @ EPLANS.COM

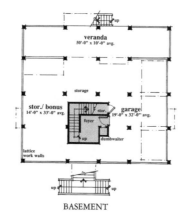

REAR EXTERIOR

Lattice walls, pickets, and horizontal siding complement a relaxed Key West design that's perfect for waterfront properties. The grand room with a fireplace, the dining room, and Bedroom 2 open through French doors to the veranda. The master suite occupies the entire second floor and features access to a private balcony through double doors. This pampering suite also includes a spacious walk-in closet and a full bath with a whirlpool tub. Enclosed storage/bonus space and a garage are available on the lower level.

master
14'-6" x 15'-6"
vault. clg.

am kitchen

down

SECOND FLOOR

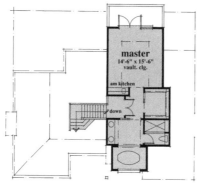

veranda
50'-0" x 10'-0" avg.

up

storage

stor./ bonus
14'-0" x 33'-0" avg.

stor.

garage
19'-0" x 32'-0" avg.

foyer

up

dumbwaiter

lattice
work walls

up   up

BASEMENT

down

veranda
50'-0" x 10'-0"

dining
12'-0" x 14'-0"
vault. clg.

kitchen
10' x 13'

br. 2
13'-0" x 13'-8"
8' clg.

grand room
15'-0" x 27'-0"
vault. clg.

down

fireplace

up

foyer

util.

down

br. 3
13'-0" x 11'-0"
8' clg.

FIRST FLOOR

ORDER BLUEPRINTS 24 HOURS, 7 DAYS A WEEK, AT 1-800-521-6797

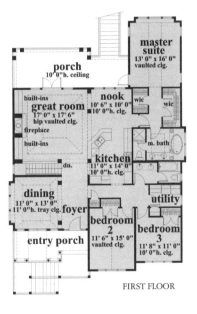

FIRST FLOOR

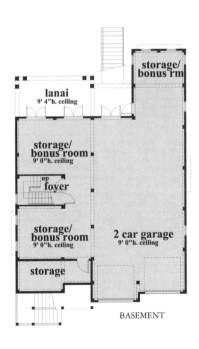

BASEMENT

plan# HPK0200036

STYLE: SEASIDE
SQUARE FOOTAGE: 2,136
BONUS SPACE: 1,428 SQ. FT.
BEDROOMS: 3
BATHROOMS: 2
WIDTH: 44' - 0"
DEPTH: 63' - 0"
FOUNDATION: ISLAND BASEMENT

SEARCH ONLINE @ EPLANS.COM

This raised Tidewater design is well suited for many building situations, with comfortable outdoor areas that encourage year-round living. Horizontal siding and a steeply pitched roof call up a sense of the past, and a smart-space interior redefines the luxury of comfort with up-to-the-minute amenities. A vaulted ceiling highlights the great room, made comfy by a centered fireplace, extensive built-ins, and French doors that let in fresh air and sunlight. The formal dining room opens from the entry hall and features a triple-window view of the side property. A secluded sitting area in the master suite features a wide window and a door to a private area of the rear porch. Two secondary bedrooms share a full bath.

RISE TO THE OCCASION
HILLSIDE LIVING AND ELEVATED FOUNDATIONS

plan# HPK0200037

STYLE: TIDEWATER
FIRST FLOOR: 2,146 SQ. FT.
SECOND FLOOR: 952 SQ. FT.
TOTAL: 3,098 SQ. FT.
BEDROOMS: 3
BATHROOMS: 3½
WIDTH: 52' - 0"
DEPTH: 65' - 4"
FOUNDATION: ISLAND BASEMENT

SEARCH ONLINE @ EPLANS.COM

Outdoor spaces, such as the inviting wraparound porch and the rear veranda, are the living areas of this cottage. French doors, a fireplace, and built-in cabinets adorn the great room. A private hall leads to the first-floor master suite. The upper level boasts a catwalk that overlooks the great room and the foyer. A secluded master wing enjoys a bumped-out window, a stunning tray ceiling, and two walk-in closets. The island kitchen conveniently accesses the nook, dining area, and the wet bar.

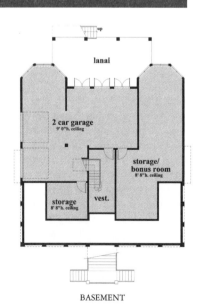

BASEMENT

FIRST FLOOR

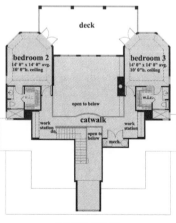

SECOND FLOOR

RISE TO THE OCCASION
HILLSIDE LIVING AND ELEVATED FOUNDATIONS

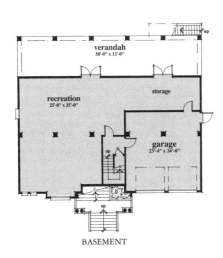

REAR EXTERIOR

plan# HPK0200038

STYLE: SEASIDE
SQUARE FOOTAGE: 2,190
BEDROOMS: 3
BATHROOMS: 2
WIDTH: 60' - 0"
DEPTH: 54' - 0"
FOUNDATION: ISLAND BASEMENT

SEARCH ONLINE @ EPLANS.COM

The dramatic arched entry of this cottage borrows freely from the Southern coastal tradition. The foyer and central hall open to the grand room. The kitchen is flanked by the dining room and the morning nook, which opens to the lanai. On the left side of the plan, the master suite also accesses the lanai. Two walk-in closets and a compartmented bath with a separate tub and shower and a double-bowl vanity complete this opulent retreat. The right side of the plan includes two secondary bedrooms and a full bath.

SECOND FLOOR

lanai
58'-0" x 10'-8"

master suite
13'-0" x 15'-0"
9'-4" stepped clg.

built ins

grand room
20'-0" x 18'-0" avg.
tray ceiling

nook
11'-0" x 9'-4"

br. 2
12'-0" x 11'-4"
9'-4" flat clg.

fireplace

built ins

kitchen
11' x 11'

eating bar

hers

his

arch

arch

utility

arch

study
11'-0" x 11'-0"
9'-4" flat clg.

foyer

down

dining
10'-10" x 15'-0"
9'-4" flat clg.

br. 3
12'-0" x 11'-0"
9'-4" flat clg.

dn.

entry porch

planter

BASEMENT

up

verandah
58'-0" x 12'-0"

recreation
25'-0" x 35'-0"

storage

up

garage
23'-4" x 24'-0"

up

RISE TO THE OCCASION
HILLSIDE LIVING AND ELEVATED FOUNDATIONS

plan # HPK0200039

STYLE: TIDEWATER
FIRST FLOOR: 1,342 SQ. FT.
SECOND FLOOR: 511 SQ. FT.
TOTAL: 1,853 SQ. FT.
BEDROOMS: 3
BATHROOMS: 2
WIDTH: 44' - 0"
DEPTH: 40' - 0"
FOUNDATION: ISLAND BASEMENT

SEARCH ONLINE @ EPLANS.COM

Detailed fretwork complements a standing-seam roof on this tropical cottage. An arch-top transom provides an absolutely perfect highlight to the classic clapboard facade. An unrestrained floor plan offers cool digs for kicking back and a sensational retreat for guests—whether the occasion is formal or casual. French doors open to a rear porch from the great room letting in fresh air and the sights and sounds of the great outdoors. Inside, the master bedroom leads to a dressing space with linen storage and a walk-in closet. The lavish bath includes a garden tub, oversized shower, and a wraparound vanity with two sinks. Two secondary bedrooms on the upper level share a spacious loft that overlooks the great room. One of the bedrooms opens to a private deck.

SECOND FLOOR

FIRST FLOOR

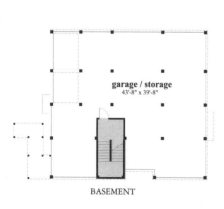

BASEMENT

RISE TO THE OCCASION
HILLSIDE LIVING AND ELEVATED FOUNDATIONS

Get away to this island of luxury—two or three family bedrooms and one enormous master suite should provide plenty of room for the entire crew. Enter the foyer via French doors to gain easy access to all levels. The basement level accesses a covered patio and allows future space for a summer kitchen, game room, home office, media room, and a guest suite with an adjacent bath. Entertaining will be easy with the gathering room, dining area, and Florida room that are open to one another and adjoin the rear covered patio. The master suite and a hobby room occupy the second level. An enormous walk-in closet, sumptuous bath, and roomy private deck enhance the master bedroom.

plan # HPK0200040

STYLE: SEASIDE
MAIN LEVEL: 2,350 SQ. FT.
UPPER LEVEL: 1,338 SQ. FT.
LOWER LEVEL: 1,509 SQ. FT.
TOTAL: 5,197 SQ. FT.
BEDROOMS: 4
BATHROOMS: 4½
DEPTH: 72' - 0"
FOUNDATION: SLAB

SEARCH ONLINE @ EPLANS.COM

LOWER LEVEL

MAIN LEVEL

UPPER LEVEL

RISE TO THE OCCASION
HILLSIDE LIVING AND ELEVATED FOUNDATIONS

plan # HPK0200041

STYLE: SEASIDE
SQUARE FOOTAGE: 3,074
BEDROOMS: 3
BATHROOMS: 3½
WIDTH: 77' - 0"
DEPTH: 66' - 8"
FOUNDATION: ISLAND BASEMENT

SEARCH ONLINE @ EPLANS.COM

Symmetry and the perfect blend of past and future mark this home. A steeply pitched roof caps a collection of Prairie-style windows and elegant columns. The portico leads to a midlevel foyer, which rises to the grand salon. A wide-open leisure room hosts a corner fireplace that's ultracozy. The master wing sprawls from the front portico to the rear covered porch, rich with luxury amenities and plenty of secluded space.

FIRST FLOOR

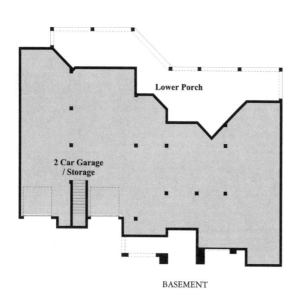

BASEMENT

RISE TO THE OCCASION
HILLSIDE LIVING AND ELEVATED FOUNDATIONS

REAR EXTERIOR

SECOND FLOOR

plan # HPK0200042

STYLE: SEASIDE
FIRST FLOOR: 1,383 SQ. FT.
SECOND FLOOR: 595 SQ. FT.
TOTAL: 1,978 SQ. FT.
BONUS SPACE: 617 SQ. FT.
BEDROOMS: 3
BATHROOMS: 2
WIDTH: 48' - 0"
DEPTH: 42' - 0"
FOUNDATION: ISLAND BASEMENT

SEARCH ONLINE @ EPLANS.COM

This fabulous Key West home blends interior space with the great outdoors. Designed for a balmy climate, this home boasts expansive porches and decks—with outside access from every area of the home. A sun-dappled foyer leads via a stately midlevel staircase to a splendid great room, which features a warming fireplace tucked in beside beautiful built-in cabinetry. Highlighted by a wall of glass that opens to the rear porch, this two-story living space opens to the formal dining room and a well-appointed kitchen. Spacious secondary bedrooms on the main level open to outside spaces and share a full bath. Upstairs, a 10-foot tray ceiling highlights a private master suite, which provides French doors to an upper-level porch.

BASEMENT

FIRST FLOOR

RISE TO THE OCCASION
HILLSIDE LIVING AND ELEVATED FOUNDATIONS

REAR EXTERIOR

plan# HPK0200043

STYLE: CONTEMPORARY
FIRST FLOOR: 876 SQ. FT.
SECOND FLOOR: 1,245 SQ. FT.
TOTAL: 2,121 SQ. FT.
BEDROOMS: 4
BATHROOMS: 2½
WIDTH: 27' - 6"
DEPTH: 64' - 0"
FOUNDATION: CRAWLSPACE

SEARCH ONLINE @ EPLANS.COM

Key West Conch style blends Old World charm with New World comfort in this picturesque design. A glass-paneled entry lends a warm welcome and complements a captivating front balcony. Two sets of French doors open the great room to wide views and extend the living areas to the back covered porch. A gourmet kitchen is prepared for any occasion with a prep sink, plenty of counter space, an ample pantry, and an eating bar. The midlevel landing leads to two additional bedrooms, a full bath, and a windowed art niche. Double French doors open the upper-level master suite to a sundeck.

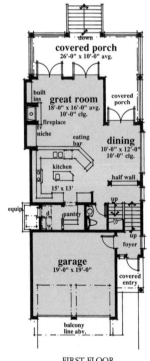

FIRST FLOOR

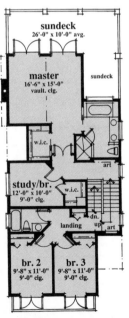

SECOND FLOOR

RISE TO THE OCCASION
HILLSIDE LIVING AND ELEVATED FOUNDATIONS

© 1998 Donald A. Gardner, Inc.

With an elevated pier foundation, this stunning home is perfect for waterfront properties. Magnificent porches, a balcony and a plethora of picture windows take advantage of the beach or lakeside views. The great room features a ten-foot beam ceiling, a fireplace and a space-saving built-in entertainment center. The staircase is highlighted by a grand window with an arched top, while a Palladian window accents the upstairs loft/study. The master bedroom is the essence of luxury with skylights, a fireplace, cathedral ceiling, balcony, vaulted bath and oversized walk-in closet. Family bedrooms on the first floor share a full bath. Note the front and rear wrapping porches.

plan # HPK0200044

STYLE: VACATION
FIRST FLOOR: 1,366 SQ. FT.
SECOND FLOOR: 689 SQ. FT.
TOTAL: 2,055 SQ. FT.
BEDROOMS: 3
BATHROOMS: 2
WIDTH: 49' - 4"
DEPTH: 50' - 4"

SEARCH ONLINE @ EPLANS.COM

FIRST FLOOR

SECOND FLOOR

RISE TO THE OCCASION
HILLSIDE LIVING AND ELEVATED FOUNDATIONS

plan # HPK0200045

STYLE: GREEK REVIVAL
FIRST FLOOR: 2,331 SQ. FT.
SECOND FLOOR: 988 SQ. FT.
TOTAL: 3,319 SQ. FT.
BEDROOMS: 3
BATHROOMS: 2½
WIDTH: 53' - 10"
DEPTH: 71' - 10"
FOUNDATION: PIER

SEARCH ONLINE @ EPLANS.COM

History-rich details lovingly rethink tradition throughout this waterfront plan to form a new notion of home and create comfort. The strength of the design lies in its simplicity, with an open interior and plenty of breezy outdoor spaces. Walls of energy-efficient glass filter sunlight to the heart of the home and allow generous views of the landscape. A gallery provides guest amenities, such as a powder room. A servery area with its own walk-in pantry links a well-equipped kitchen to the formal dining room. French doors lead from the master suite and morning area to an extensive outdoor space that includes a covered porch. Upstairs, a wraparound loft leads to an open library.

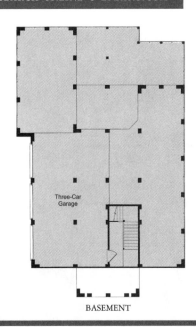

BASEMENT

FIRST FLOOR

SECOND FLOOR

plan# HPK0200046

STYLE: COUNTRY COTTAGE
FIRST FLOOR: 2,390 SQ. FT.
SECOND FLOOR: 1,200 SQ. FT.
TOTAL: 3,590 SQ. FT.
BEDROOMS: 4
BATHROOMS: 3
WIDTH: 61' - 0"
DEPTH: 64' - 4"
FOUNDATION: ISLAND BASEMENT

SEARCH ONLINE @ EPLANS.COM

This luxurious waterfront design sings of Southern island influences. A front covered porch opens to a foyer, flanked by a study and dining room. The living room, warmed by a fireplace and safe from off-season ocean breezes, overlooks the rear covered porch. The island kitchen extends into a break-fast room. Beyond the covered porch, the wood deck is also accessed privately from the master suite. This suite includes a private whirlpool bath and huge walk-in closet. A guest suite is located on the first floor, while two additional bedrooms and a multimedia room are located on the second level.

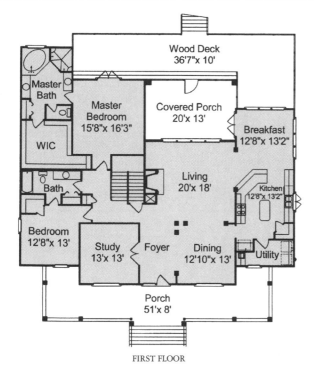

FIRST FLOOR

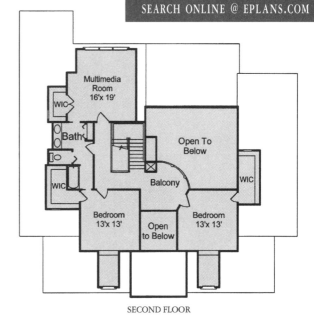

SECOND FLOOR

RISE TO THE OCCASION
HILLSIDE LIVING AND ELEVATED FOUNDATIONS

plan(#) HPK0200047

STYLE: TIDEWATER
FIRST FLOOR: 1,855 SQ. FT.
SECOND FLOOR: 901 SQ. FT.
TOTAL: 2,756 SQ. FT.
BEDROOMS: 3
BATHROOMS: 3½
WIDTH: 66' - 0"
DEPTH: 50' - 0"
FOUNDATION: ISLAND BASEMENT

SEARCH ONLINE @ EPLANS.COM

This Southern tidewater cottage is the perfect vacation hideaway. An octagonal great room with a multifaceted vaulted ceiling illuminates the interior. The island kitchen is brightened by a bumped-out window and a pass-through to the lanai. Two walk-in closets and a whirlpool bath await to indulge the homeowner in the master suite. A set of double doors opens to the vaulted master lanai for quiet comfort. The U-shaped staircase leads to a loft, which overlooks the great room and the foyer. Two additional family bedrooms offer private baths. A computer center and a morning kitchen complete the upper level.

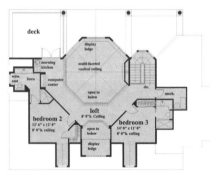

SECOND FLOOR

FIRST FLOOR

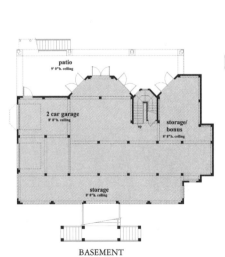

BASEMENT

This charming country home features a rocking-chair porch. The foyer area is brightened by the light from one of the home's three dormers. Another dormer gives light to the optional loft at the top of the stairs. The modified cathedral ceiling of the living area frames the fireplace wall for a dramatic effect. Three bay windows highlight the house adding space and light to the dining and breakfast areas and create a sitting area in the master suite. This drive-under basement design fits snugly on side sloping lots.

plan # HPK0200048

STYLE: COLONIAL
SQUARE FOOTAGE: 1,721
BEDROOMS: 3
BATHROOMS: 2
WIDTH: 56' - 4"
DEPTH: 44' - 0"
FOUNDATION: BASEMENT

SEARCH ONLINE @ EPLANS.COM

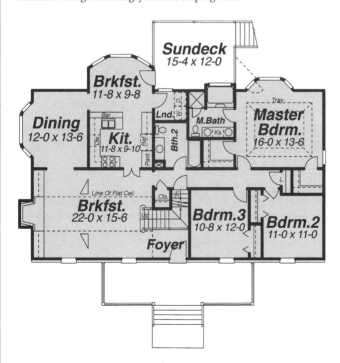

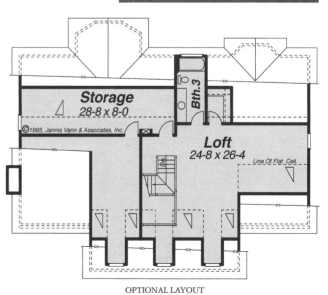

OPTIONAL LAYOUT

RISE TO THE OCCASION
HILLSIDE LIVING AND ELEVATED FOUNDATIONS

plan# HPK0200049

STYLE: LAKESIDE
FIRST FLOOR: 1,143 SQ. FT.
SECOND FLOOR: 651 SQ. FT.
TOTAL: 1,794 SQ. FT.
BONUS SPACE: 651 SQ. FT.
BEDROOMS: 2
BATHROOMS: 2½
WIDTH: 32' - 0"
DEPTH: 57' - 0"
FOUNDATION: BASEMENT

SEARCH ONLINE @ EPLANS.COM

REAR EXTERIOR

This traditional country cabin is a vacationer's dream. Stone and vertical wood siding rustically camouflage the exterior; the inside pampers in lavish style. An elegant entryway extends into the foyer, where straight ahead, the two-story great room visually expands the lofty interior. This room provides a warming fireplace and offers built-in cabinetry. Double doors open to a fresh veranda, which wraps around to the rear deck—a perfect place to enjoy the outdoors. Upstairs, a vaulted ceiling enhances the master suite and its private bath. A private deck from the master suite can be accessed through a set of double doors. The loft area overlooking the great room accesses a second deck. The basement level hosts a bonus room, storage area, and two-car garage.

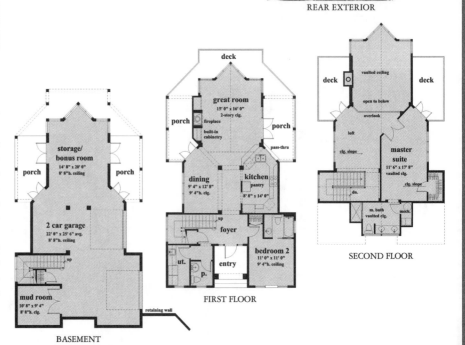

BASEMENT

FIRST FLOOR

SECOND FLOOR

RISE TO THE OCCASION
HILLSIDE LIVING AND ELEVATED FOUNDATIONS

Stonework and elements of Craftsman style make a strong statement but are partnered here with a sweet disposition. Sidelights and transoms enrich the elevation and offer a warm welcome to a well-accoutered interior with up-to-the-minute amenities. A wealth of windows allows gentle breezes to flow through the living space, and French doors extend an invitation to enjoy the rear covered porch. Nearby, a well-organized kitchen offers a pass-through to the great room, and service to the formal dining room through a convenient butler's pantry. Upstairs, the master suite sports a private sitting area that opens to an upper deck through French doors. The upper-level gallery provides an overlook to the great room and connects the master retreat with a secondary bedroom that opens to the deck.

plan # HPK0200050

STYLE: RUSTIC COUNTRY
FIRST FLOOR: 1,542 SQ. FT.
SECOND FLOOR: 971 SQ. FT.
TOTAL: 2,513 SQ. FT.
BEDROOMS: 3
BATHROOMS: 3
WIDTH: 46' - 0"
DEPTH: 51' - 0"
FOUNDATION: ISLAND BASEMENT

SEARCH ONLINE @ EPLANS.COM

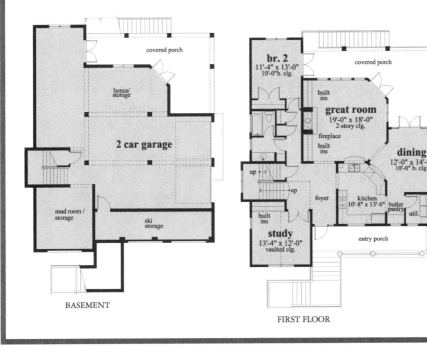

BASEMENT

FIRST FLOOR

SECOND FLOOR

RISE TO THE OCCASION
HILLSIDE LIVING AND ELEVATED FOUNDATIONS

plan # HPK0200051

STYLE: HILLSIDE
FIRST FLOOR: 1,022 SQ. FT.
SECOND FLOOR: 813 SQ. FT.
TOTAL: 1,835 SQ. FT.
BEDROOMS: 3
BATHROOMS: 2½
WIDTH: 36' - 0"
DEPTH: 33' - 0"
FOUNDATION: SLAB

SEARCH ONLINE @ EPLANS.COM

This home is quite a "looker" with its steeply sloping rooflines and large sunburst and multipane windows. This plan not only accommodates a narrow lot, but it also fits a sloping site. The angled corner entry gives way to a two-story living room with a tiled hearth. The dining room shares an interesting angled space with this area and enjoys easy service from the efficient kitchen. The family room offers double doors to a refreshing balcony. A powder room and laundry room complete the main level. Upstairs, a vaulted master bedroom enjoys a private bath; two other bedrooms share a bath.

FIRST FLOOR

SECOND FLOOR

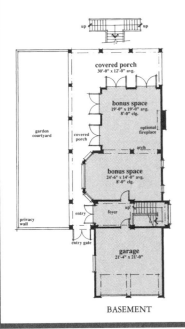

REAR EXTERIOR

plan# HPK0200052

STYLE: TIDEWATER
FIRST FLOOR: 1,305 SQ. FT.
SECOND FLOOR: 1,215 SQ. FT.
TOTAL: 2,520 SQ. FT.
BONUS SPACE: 935 SQ. FT.
BEDROOMS: 3
BATHROOMS: 3
WIDTH: 30' - 6"
DEPTH: 72' - 2"
FOUNDATION: ISLAND BASEMENT

SEARCH ONLINE @ EPLANS.COM

SECOND FLOOR

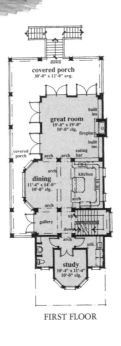

BASEMENT

FIRST FLOOR

This elegant Old Charleston Row design blends high vogue with a restful character that says shoes are optional. A flexible interior enjoys modern space that welcomes sunlight. Wraparound porticos on two levels offer views to the living areas, and a "sit-and-watch-the-stars" observation deck opens from the master suite. Four sets of French doors bring the outside into the great room. The second-floor master suite features a spacious bath and three sets of doors that open to the observation deck. A guest bedroom on this level leads to a gallery hall with its own access to the deck. Bonus space awaits development on the lower level, which—true to its Old Charleston roots—opens gloriously to a garden courtyard.

RISE TO THE OCCASION
HILLSIDE LIVING AND ELEVATED FOUNDATIONS

plan # HPK0200053

STYLE: TIDEWATER
FIRST FLOOR: 1,046 SQ. FT.
SECOND FLOOR: 638 SQ. FT.
TOTAL: 1,684 SQ. FT.
BEDROOMS: 3
BATHROOMS: 3
WIDTH: 25' - 0"
DEPTH: 65' - 6"
FOUNDATION: CRAWLSPACE

SEARCH ONLINE @ EPLANS.COM

This cozy retreat offers bright and airy living areas and covered porches. Built-ins and a media niche frame the great-room fireplace. Four sets of French doors in the great room access the covered wraparound porch. The gourmet kitchen shares an eating bar with the great room and is open to the dining room through a hallway with arches. A first-floor bedroom with a built-in desk easily accesses the full hall bath. The second floor contains an observation deck, the master suite with a grand private bath and walk-in closet, plus a third bedroom with a private bath and window seat.

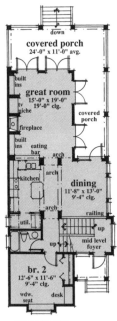

FIRST FLOOR

REAR EXTERIOR

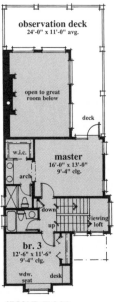

SECOND FLOOR

RISE TO THE OCCASION
HILLSIDE LIVING AND ELEVATED FOUNDATIONS

This charming Charleston design is full of surprises! Perfect for a narrow footprint, the raised foundation is ideal for a waterfront location. An entry porch introduces a winding staircase. To the right is a living room/library that functions as a formal entertaining space. A large hearth and two sets of French doors to the covered porch enhance the great room. The master suite is positioned for privacy and includes great amenities that work to relax the homeowners. Upstairs, three family bedrooms, two full baths, an open media room, and a future game room create a fantastic casual family space.

plan# HPK0200054

STYLE: TIDEWATER
FIRST FLOOR: 2,578 SQ. FT.
SECOND FLOOR: 1,277 SQ. FT.
TOTAL: 3,855 SQ. FT.
BEDROOMS: 4
BATHROOMS: 4
WIDTH: 53' - 6"
DEPTH: 97' - 0"
FOUNDATION: ISLAND BASEMENT

SEARCH ONLINE @ EPLANS.COM

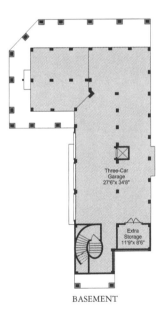

BASEMENT

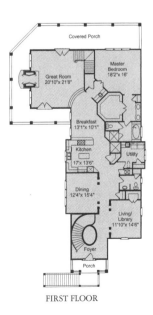

FIRST FLOOR

SECOND FLOOR

RISE TO THE OCCASION
HILLSIDE LIVING AND ELEVATED FOUNDATIONS

© 1998 Donald A Gardner, Inc.
B. NATHAN

plan # HPK0200055

STYLE: CRAFTSMAN
FIRST FLOOR: 1,650 SQ. FT.
SECOND FLOOR: 712 SQ. FT.
TOTAL: 2,362 SQ. FT.
BEDROOMS: 3
BATHROOMS: 2½
WIDTH: 58' - 10"
DEPTH: 47' - 4"

SEARCH ONLINE @ EPLANS.COM

Cedar shakes and striking gables with decorative scalloped insets adorn the exterior of this lovely coastal home. The generous great room is expanded by a rear wall of windows, with additional light from transom windows above the front door and a rear clerestory dormer. The kitchen features a pass-through to the great room. The dining room, great room, and study all access an inviting back porch. The master bedroom is a treat with a private balcony, His and Hers walk-in closets, and an impeccable bath. Upstairs, a room-sized loft with an arched opening overlooks the great room below. Two more bedrooms, one with its own private balcony, share a hall bath.

FIRST FLOOR

SECOND FLOOR

RISE TO THE OCCASION
HILLSIDE LIVING AND ELEVATED FOUNDATIONS

B. NATHAN

©1999 Donald A. Gardner, Inc.

REAR EXTERIOR

©1999 Donald A. Gardner, Inc.

MAIN LEVEL

LOWER LEVEL

plan# HPK0200056

STYLE: CRAFTSMAN
MAIN LEVEL: 2,068 SQ. FT.
LOWER LEVEL: 930 SQ. FT.
TOTAL: 2,998 SQ. FT.
BEDROOMS: 3
BATHROOMS: 3½
DEPTH: 66' - 0"

SEARCH ONLINE @ EPLANS.COM

This Craftsman-style home takes advantage of hillside views with its deck, patio, and an abundance of rear windows. An open floor plan enhances the home's spaciousness. The great room features a cathedral ceiling, a fireplace with built-in cabinets and shelves, and access to the generous rear deck. Designed for ultimate efficiency, the kitchen serves the great room, dining room, and breakfast area with equal ease. A tray ceiling lends elegance to the master bedroom, which features deck access, twin walk-in closets, and an extravagant bath with dual vanities, a large linen closet, and separate tub and shower.

RISE TO THE OCCASION
HILLSIDE LIVING AND ELEVATED FOUNDATIONS

plan # HPK0200057

STYLE: COUNTRY
FIRST FLOOR: 1,620 SQ. FT.
SECOND FLOOR: 770 SQ. FT.
TOTAL: 2,390 SQ. FT.
BEDROOMS: 3
BATHROOMS: 3½
WIDTH: 49' - 0"
DEPTH: 58' - 8"

SEARCH ONLINE @ EPLANS.COM

Multiple gables, a center dormer with arched clerestory window, and a striking front staircase create visual excitement for this three-bedroom coastal home. Vaulted ceilings in the foyer and great room highlight a dramatic second-floor balcony that connects the two upstairs bedrooms, each with its own bath and private porch. The great room is generously proportioned with built-ins on either side of the fireplace. Private back porches enhance the dining room and the master suite, which boasts His and Hers walk-in closets and a magnificent bath with dual vanities, a garden tub, and separate shower.

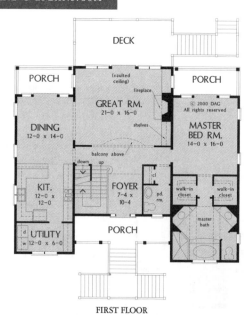

FIRST FLOOR

SECOND FLOOR

©1998 Donald A. Gardner, Inc.

REAR EXTERIOR

plan# HPK0200058

STYLE: COUNTRY
MAIN LEVEL: 2,065 SQ. FT.
LOWER LEVEL: 1,216 SQ. FT.
TOTAL: 3,281 SQ. FT.
BEDROOMS: 4
BATHROOMS: 3½
DEPTH: 43' - 6"

SEARCH ONLINE @ EPLANS.COM

MAIN LEVEL

LOWER LEVEL

Stone, siding, and multiple gables combine beautifully on the exterior of this hillside home. Taking advantage of rear views, the home's most oft-used rooms are oriented at the back with plenty of windows. Augmented by a cathedral ceiling, the great room features a fireplace, built-in shelves, and access to the rear deck. Twin walk-in closets and a private bath infuse the master suite with luxury. The nearby powder room offers an optional full-bath arrangement, allowing the study to double as a bedroom. Downstairs, a large media/recreation room with a wet bar and fireplace separates two more bedrooms, each with a full bath and walk-in closet.

RISE TO THE OCCASION
HILLSIDE LIVING AND ELEVATED FOUNDATIONS

© 1999 Donald A. Gardner, Inc.

plan# HPK0200059

STYLE: HILLSIDE
MAIN LEVEL: 2,122 SQ. FT.
LOWER LEVEL: 1,150 SQ. FT.
TOTAL: 3,272 SQ. FT.
BEDROOMS: 4
BATHROOMS: 3
DEPTH: 74' - 4"

SEARCH ONLINE @ EPLANS.COM

A Craftsman combination of cedar shingles and wood siding lends warmth and style to this four-bedroom home. A stunning cathedral ceiling spans the open great room and spacious island kitchen for exceptional volume. A deep tray ceiling heightens the formal dining room, while the breakfast room is enhanced by a vaulted ceiling. Two rear decks and a screened porch augment the home's ample living space. The master bedroom is topped by a tray ceiling and features two walk-in closets and a generous private bath. A second bedroom is located on the main level and two more can be found on the lower level.

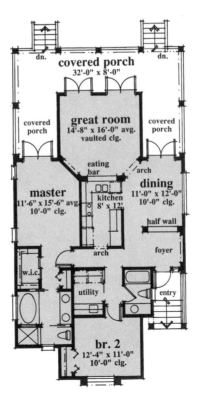

REAR EXTERIOR

plan# HPK0200060

STYLE: TIDEWATER
SQUARE FOOTAGE: 1,288
BEDROOMS: 2
BATHROOMS: 2
WIDTH: 32' - 4"
DEPTH: 60' - 0"
FOUNDATION: CRAWLSPACE

SEARCH ONLINE @ EPLANS.COM

Welcome home to casual, unstuffy living with this comfortable tidewater design. The heart of this home is the great room, where a put-your-feet-up atmosphere prevails, and the dusky hues of sunset can mingle with the sounds of ocean breakers. An efficiently designed kitchen opens to a dining room that accesses the rear porch. French doors open the master suite to a private area of the covered porch, where sunlight and sea breezes mingle with a spirit of bon vivant.

THE PERFECT GETAWAY
RUSTIC COTTAGES AND VACATION HOMES

This sweet lakeside cottage is sure to please with its quaint charm and convenient floor plan. A covered porch greets family and friends and offers a place to sit and enjoy the summer breezes. Inside, the living room—with its warming fireplace—flows nicely into the kitchen/dining area. A snack bar, pantry, and plenty of cabinet and counter space are just some of the features found here. The first-floor master suite includes a bay window, walk-in closet, and private bath. Upstairs, two bedrooms share a bath and linen closet.

SECOND FLOOR

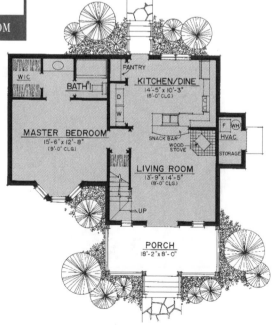

FIRST FLOOR

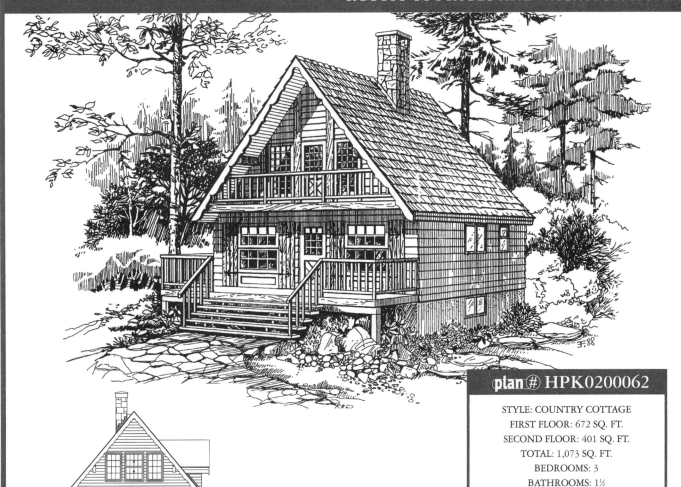

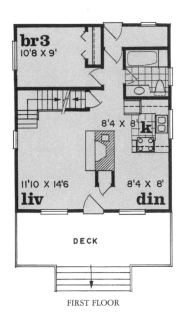

REAR EXTERIOR

plan# HPK0200062

STYLE: COUNTRY COTTAGE
FIRST FLOOR: 672 SQ. FT.
SECOND FLOOR: 401 SQ. FT.
TOTAL: 1,073 SQ. FT.
BEDROOMS: 3
BATHROOMS: 1½
WIDTH: 24' - 0"
DEPTH: 36' - 0"
FOUNDATION: CRAWLSPACE, BASEMENT

SEARCH ONLINE @ EPLANS.COM

This chalet plan is enhanced by a steep gable roof, scalloped fascia boards, and fieldstone chimney detail. The front-facing deck and covered balcony add to outdoor living spaces. The fireplace is the main focus in the living room. The bedroom on the first floor enjoys access to a full hall bath. A storage/mudroom at the back of the plan is perfect for keeping skis and boots. Two additional bedrooms and a half-bath occupy the second floor. The master bedroom provides a walk-in closet. Three storage areas are also found on the second floor.

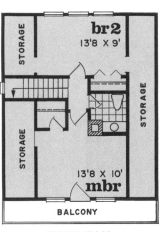

FIRST FLOOR

SECOND FLOOR

THE PERFECT GETAWAY
RUSTIC COTTAGES AND VACATION HOMES

plan# HPK0200063

STYLE: EUROPEAN COTTAGE
FIRST FLOOR: 665 SQ. FT.
SECOND FLOOR: 395 SQ. FT.
TOTAL: 1,060 SQ. FT.
BEDROOMS: 1
BATHROOMS: 1
WIDTH: 34' - 3"
DEPTH: 32' - 5"
FOUNDATION: SLAB

SEARCH ONLINE @ EPLANS.COM

With woodsy charm and cozy livability, this cottage plan offers comfortable living space in a smaller footprint. The exterior is geared for outdoor fun, with two flagstone patios connected by a two-way fireplace and graced by a built-in barbecue. French doors on two sides lead into the large playroom, which features a kitchen area, washer and dryer space, and a bath with corner sink and shower. Take the L-shaped stairway to the bunk room upstairs, where there is space for sleeping and relaxing.

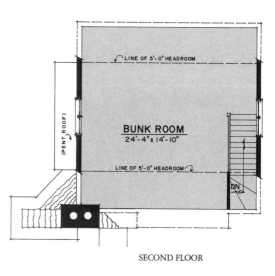

SECOND FLOOR

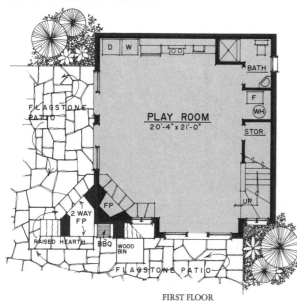

FIRST FLOOR

THE PERFECT GETAWAY
RUSTIC COTTAGES AND VACATION HOMES

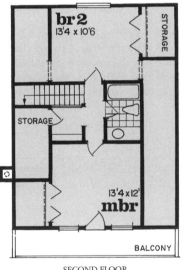

SECOND FLOOR

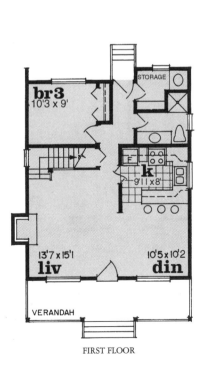

FIRST FLOOR

This cozy chalet design begins with a railed veranda opening to a living room with a warm fireplace and a dining room with a snack-bar counter through to the kitchen. The kitchen itself is U-shaped and has a sink with a window. A full bath and large storage area sit just beyond the kitchen. One bedroom is on the first floor, and the second floor holds two additional bedrooms and a full bath. The master bedroom enjoys a private balcony. Additional storage is found on the second floor.

THE PERFECT GETAWAY
RUSTIC COTTAGES AND VACATION HOMES

plan# HPK0200065

STYLE: EUROPEAN COTTAGE
FIRST FLOOR: 1,115 SQ. FT.
SECOND FLOOR: 690 SQ. FT.
TOTAL: 1,805 SQ. FT.
BEDROOMS: 3
BATHROOMS: 2
WIDTH: 43' - 0"
DEPTH: 32' - 0"
FOUNDATION: BASEMENT

SEARCH ONLINE @ EPLANS.COM

This quaint Tudor cottage has an open floor plan that is designed for easy living. The gathering room is accented with a cathedral ceiling and a full Palladian window. The dining room is joined to the efficient kitchen, with extra entertaining space available on the deck. The first-floor master suite has a large compartmented bath and bumped-out windows. Upstairs, a lounge overlooks the gathering room and accesses an outside balcony. Two additional bedrooms and a full hall bath complete the second floor.

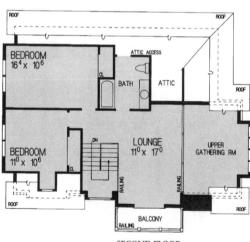

SECOND FLOOR

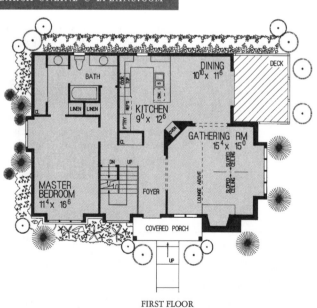

FIRST FLOOR

Nature enthusiasts are right at home in this engaging two-story home with expansive views and a delightful sunroom. The enclosed vestibule opens to the spacious living/dining room where sunlight abounds. The adjoining, U-shaped island kitchen has access to the angular sunroom for casual yet visually stimulating dining. The utility room is tucked away behind the stairs with the full bath. One bedroom is found on the first floor, and two additional bedrooms share a full bath on the second floor.

plan # HPK0200066

STYLE: SEASIDE
FIRST FLOOR: 918 SQ. FT.
SECOND FLOOR: 532 SQ. FT.
TOTAL: 1,450 SQ. FT.
BEDROOMS: 3
BATHROOMS: 2
WIDTH: 26' - 4"
DEPTH: 37' - 0"
FOUNDATION: BASEMENT

SEARCH ONLINE @ EPLANS.COM

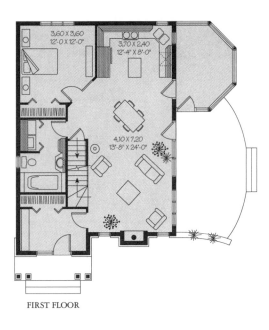

FIRST FLOOR

SECOND FLOOR

THE PERFECT GETAWAY
RUSTIC COTTAGES AND VACATION HOMES

plan # HPK0200067

STYLE: LAKEFRONT
FIRST FLOOR: 895 SQ. FT.
SECOND FLOOR: 576 SQ. FT.
TOTAL: 1,471 SQ. FT.
BEDROOMS: 3
BATHROOMS: 2
WIDTH: 26' - 0"
DEPTH: 36' - 0"
FOUNDATION: BASEMENT

SEARCH ONLINE @ EPLANS.COM

Here's a favorite waterfront home with plenty of space to kick back and relax. A lovely sunroom opens from the dining room and allows great views. An angled hearth warms the living and dining areas. Three lovely windows brighten the dining space, which leads out to a stunning sunporch. The gourmet kitchen has an island counter with a snack bar. The first-floor master bedroom enjoys a walk-in closet and a nearby bath. Upstairs, a spacious bath with a whirlpool tub is thoughtfully placed between two bedrooms. A daylight basement allows a lower-level portico.

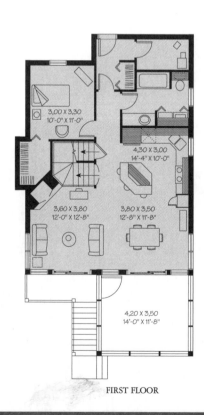

FIRST FLOOR

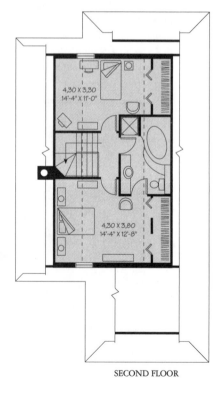

SECOND FLOOR

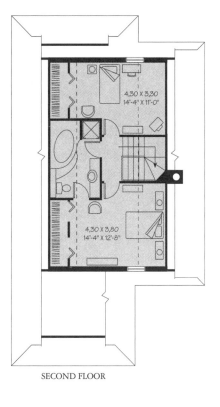

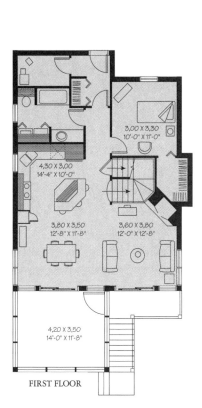

plan# HPK0200068

STYLE: LAKEFRONT
FIRST FLOOR: 895 SQ. FT.
SECOND FLOOR: 576 SQ. FT.
TOTAL: 1,471 SQ. FT.
BEDROOMS: 3
BATHROOMS: 2
WIDTH: 26' - 0"
DEPTH: 36' - 0"
FOUNDATION: BASEMENT

SEARCH ONLINE @ EPLANS.COM

This vacation home enjoys a screened porch that sits on stilts. Truly a free-flowing plan, the dining room, living room, and kitchen share a common space, with no walls separating them. An island snack counter in the kitchen provides plenty of space for food preparation. A family bedroom and full bath complete the first level. Upstairs, two additional bedrooms—with ample closet space—share a lavish bath, which includes a whirlpool tub and separate shower.

SECOND FLOOR

FIRST FLOOR

THE PERFECT GETAWAY
RUSTIC COTTAGES AND VACATION HOMES

plan# HPK0200069

STYLE: VACATION
FIRST FLOOR: 858 SQ. FT.
SECOND FLOOR: 502 SQ. FT.
TOTAL: 1,360 SQ. FT.
BEDROOMS: 3
BATHROOMS: 2
WIDTH: 35' - 0"
DEPTH: 29' - 8"
FOUNDATION: BASEMENT

SEARCH ONLINE @ EPLANS.COM

This fine brick home features a bay-windowed sunroom, perfect for admiring the view. Inside this open floor plan, a family room features a fireplace and a spacious eat-in kitchen with access to the sunroom. A bedroom, full bath, and laundry facilities complete this floor. Upstairs, two more bedrooms share a compartmented bath, as well as an overlook to the family room below.

REAR EXTERIOR

FIRST FLOOR

SECOND FLOOR

THE PERFECT GETAWAY
RUSTIC COTTAGES AND VACATION HOMES

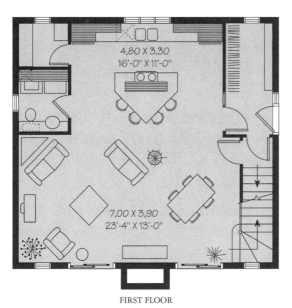

This stunning contemporary cottage has a heart of gold, with plenty of windows to bring in a wealth of natural light. Open planning allows the first-floor living and dining room to share the wide views of the outdoors. Glass doors frame the fireplace and open to the deck. A second-floor mezzanine enjoys an overlook to the living area and leads to a generous master suite with a walk-in closet, private bath, and a sitting area.

plan# HPK0200070

STYLE: COUNTRY COTTAGE
FIRST FLOOR: 728 SQ. FT.
SECOND FLOOR: 420 SQ. FT.
TOTAL: 1,148 SQ. FT.
BEDROOMS: 1
BATHROOMS: 1½
WIDTH: 28' - 0"
DEPTH: 26' - 0"
FOUNDATION: BASEMENT

SEARCH ONLINE @ EPLANS.COM

4,80 X 3,30
16'-0" X 11'-0"

7,00 X 3,90
23'-4" X 13'-0"

FIRST FLOOR

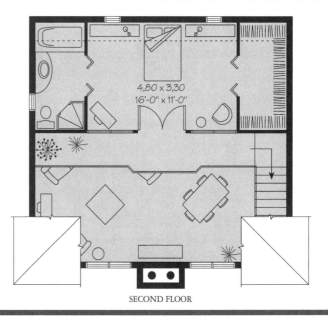

4,80 x 3,30
16'-0" x 11'-0"

SECOND FLOOR

THE PERFECT GETAWAY
RUSTIC COTTAGES AND VACATION HOMES

plan # HPK0200071

STYLE: COUNTRY COTTAGE
FIRST FLOOR: 784 SQ. FT.
SECOND FLOOR: 275 SQ. FT.
TOTAL: 1,059 SQ. FT.
BEDROOMS: 2
BATHROOMS: 1
WIDTH: 32' - 0"
DEPTH: 30' - 0"
FOUNDATION: CRAWLSPACE

SEARCH ONLINE @ EPLANS.COM

This chalet-style vacation home, with its steep, overhanging roof, will catch the eye of every envious neighbor. It is designed to be completely livable whether it's the season for swimming or skiing. The dormitory on the upper level will sleep many vacationers; two bedrooms on the first floor provide more conventional sleeping facilities. The upper level overlooks the beamed-ceiling living and dining area. A wraparound terrace and plenty of storage space complete this perfect design.

DORMITORY
$15^8 \times 14^2$

DN
RAILING

SLOPED CEILING

GATHERING ROOM
BELOW

SECOND FLOOR

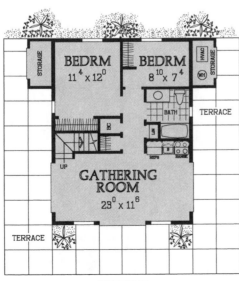

STORAGE

BEDRM
$11^4 \times 12^0$

BEDRM
$8^{10} \times 7^4$

HVAC
STORAGE
WH

BATH

TERRACE

UP

GATHERING ROOM
$23^0 \times 11^6$

TERRACE

FIRST FLOOR

This A-frame cottage takes advantage of a front view from a deck and a balcony. The open living and dining rooms are warmed by a woodstove and stretch out to enjoy the deck. The master bedroom is to the rear and has a walk-in closet and a powder room nearby. Two bedrooms upstairs have large wall closets and share a full bath. Bedroom 3 has two doors to the balcony.

plan # HPK0200072

STYLE: VACATION
FIRST FLOOR: 780 SQ. FT.
SECOND FLOOR: 601 SQ. FT.
TOTAL: 1,381 SQ. FT.
BEDROOMS: 3
BATHROOMS: 1½
WIDTH: 26' - 0"
DEPTH: 30' - 0"
FOUNDATION: CRAWLSPACE

SEARCH ONLINE @ EPLANS.COM

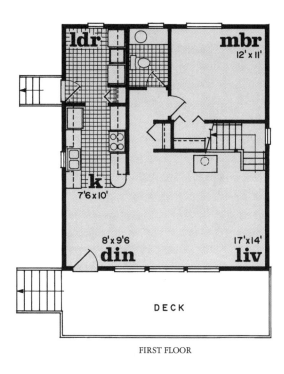

FIRST FLOOR

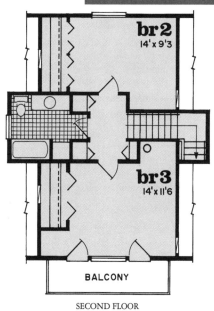

SECOND FLOOR

THE PERFECT GETAWAY
RUSTIC COTTAGES AND VACATION HOMES

plan# HPK0200073

STYLE: VACATION
FIRST FLOOR: 1,061 SQ. FT.
SECOND FLOOR: 482 SQ. FT.
TOTAL: 1,543 SQ. FT.
BEDROOMS: 3
BATHROOMS: 2
WIDTH: 28' - 0"
DEPTH: 39' - 9"
FOUNDATION: CRAWLSPACE

SEARCH ONLINE @ EPLANS.COM

A sundeck makes this design popular, but it is enhanced by views through an expansive wall of glass in the living and dining rooms. These rooms are warmed by a woodstove and enjoy vaulted ceilings as well. The kitchen is also vaulted and has a prep island and breakfast bar. Behind the kitchen is a laundry room with side-deck access. Two bedrooms and a full bath are found on the first floor. A skylit staircase leads up to the master suite and its walk-in closet and private bath on the second floor.

REAR EXTERIOR

br2 13'4 x 11'
br3 10' x 11'

liv 13'6 x 14'6 & 18'3 VAULTED

WOOD STOVE

VAULTED k 10'4 x 9'9

din 13'6 x 11'9 & 8' VAULTED

dn

SUNDECK

FIRST FLOOR

mbr 19'8 x 11'

8' CLG. LINE
4' HIGH WALL

L/T
dn BALCONY

SKYLIGHT

OPEN TO BELOW

SECOND FLOOR

ORDER BLUEPRINTS 24 HOURS, 7 DAYS A WEEK, AT 1-800-521-6797

THE PERFECT GETAWAY
RUSTIC COTTAGES AND VACATION HOMES

A surrounding sundeck and an expansive window wall capitalize on vacation-home views in this design. The full-height windows flood the living and dining rooms with abundant natural light and bring attention to the high vaulted ceilings. A woodstove in the living area warms cold winter nights. The efficient U-shaped kitchen has ample counter and cupboard space. Behind it is a laundry room and the rear entrance. The master bedroom sits on this floor and includes a large wall closet. Two family bedrooms on the second floor share a half-bath.

plan# HPK0200074

STYLE: LAKEFRONT
FIRST FLOOR: 898 SQ. FT.
SECOND FLOOR: 358 SQ. FT.
TOTAL: 1,256 SQ. FT.
BEDROOMS: 3
BATHROOMS: 1½
WIDTH: 34' - 0"
DEPTH: 32' - 0"
FOUNDATION: CRAWLSPACE

SEARCH ONLINE @ EPLANS.COM

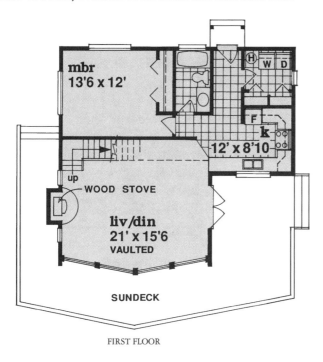

FIRST FLOOR

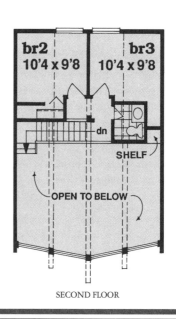

SECOND FLOOR

THE PERFECT GETAWAY
RUSTIC COTTAGES AND VACATION HOMES

plan# HPK0200075

STYLE: VACATION
SQUARE FOOTAGE: 680
BONUS SPACE: 419 SQ. FT.
BEDROOMS: 1
BATHROOMS: 1
WIDTH: 26' - 6"
DEPTH: 28' - 0"
FOUNDATION: CRAWLSPACE

SEARCH ONLINE @ EPLANS.COM

Full window walls provide the living and dining rooms of this rustic vacation home with natural light. A full sundeck with a built-in barbecue sits just outside the living area and is entered through sliding glass doors. The entire living space has a vaulted ceiling to gain spaciousness and to allow for the full-height windows. The efficient U-shaped kitchen has a pass-through counter to the dining area and a corner sink with windows overhead. A master bedroom is on the first floor and has the use of a full bath. A loft on the second floor overlooks the living room. It provides an additional 419 square feet not included in the total. Use it for an additional bedroom or as a studio.

REAR EXTERIOR

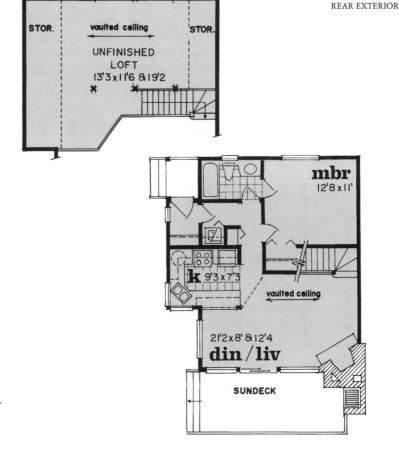

plan # HPK0200076

STYLE: NW CONTEMPORARY
FIRST FLOOR: 1,157 SQ. FT.
SECOND FLOOR: 638 SQ. FT.
TOTAL: 1,795 SQ. FT.
BEDROOMS: 3
BATHROOMS: 2½
WIDTH: 36' - 0"
DEPTH: 40' - 0"
FOUNDATION: CRAWLSPACE,
BASEMENT

SEARCH ONLINE @ EPLANS.COM

This leisure home is perfect for outdoor living, with French doors opening to a large sundeck and sunken spa. The open-beam, vaulted ceiling, and high window wall provide views for the living and dining rooms, which are decorated with wood columns and warmed by a fireplace. The step-saving U-shaped kitchen has ample counter space and a bar counter to the dining room. The master suite on the first floor features a walk-in closet and a private bath. A convenient mudroom with an adjoining laundry room accesses a rear deck. Two bedrooms on the second floor share a full bath.

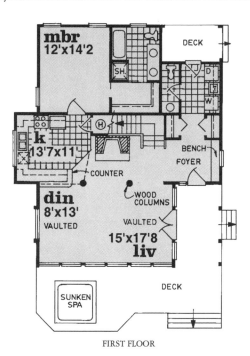

THE PERFECT GETAWAY
RUSTIC COTTAGES AND VACATION HOMES

plan# HPK0200077

STYLE: VACATION
FIRST FLOOR: 616 SQ. FT.
SECOND FLOOR: 300 SQ. FT.
TOTAL: 916 SQ. FT.
BEDROOMS: 2
BATHROOMS: 1
WIDTH: 22' - 0"
DEPTH: 28' - 0"
FOUNDATION: CRAWLSPACE

SEARCH ONLINE @ EPLANS.COM

Rustic details such as a stone fireplace work well for a country cottage such as this. A floor-to-ceiling window wall accents the living and dining rooms and provides an expansive view past a wide deck. Twin sliding glass doors access the deck from the living space. The U-shaped kitchen offers roomy counters and is open to the dining room. Behind it is a laundry room and then a full bath serving the master bedroom. An additional bedroom sits on the second floor and may be used as a studio.

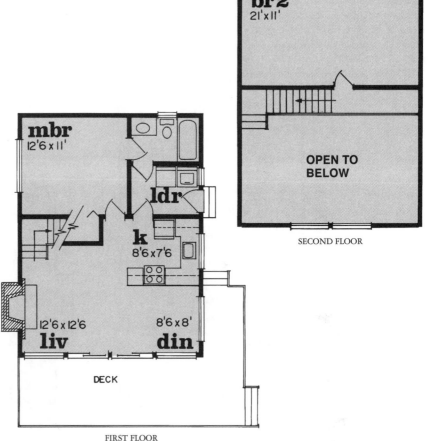

plan# HPK0200078

STYLE: VACATION
FIRST FLOOR: 1,042 SQ. FT.
SECOND FLOOR: 456 SQ. FT.
TOTAL: 1,498 SQ. FT.
BEDROOMS: 3
BATHROOMS: 2
WIDTH: 36' - 0"
DEPTH: 35' - 8"
FOUNDATION: CRAWLSPACE,
BASEMENT

SEARCH ONLINE @ EPLANS.COM

With a deck to the front, this vacation home won't miss out on any outdoor fun. The living and dining rooms are dominated by a window wall that takes advantage of the view. A high vaulted ceiling and wood-burning fireplace create a warm atmosphere. The U-shaped kitchen, with an adjoining laundry room, is open to the dining room with a pass-through counter. Note the deck beyond the kitchen and the full wall closet by the laundry. The master bedroom to the rear utilizes a full bath with a large linen closet. Two family bedrooms upstairs share a full bath that includes a skylight.

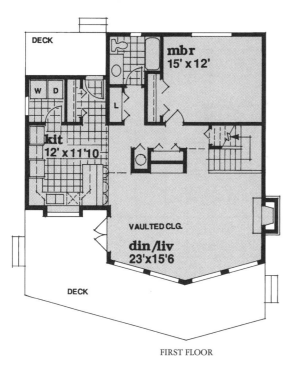

FIRST FLOOR

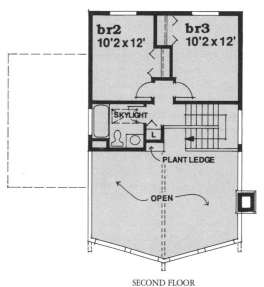

SECOND FLOOR

THE PERFECT GETAWAY
RUSTIC COTTAGES AND VACATION HOMES

REAR EXTERIOR

plan# HPK0200079

STYLE: VACATION
FIRST FLOOR: 1,197 SQ. FT.
SECOND FLOOR: 497 SQ. FT.
TOTAL: 1,694 SQ. FT.
BEDROOMS: 2
BATHROOMS: 1
WIDTH: 31' - 6"
DEPTH: 38' - 0"
FOUNDATION: BASEMENT

SEARCH ONLINE @ EPLANS.COM

A fieldstone fireplace and wrapping deck add much to the rustic beauty of this design. An expansive window wall highlights the living and dining room's vaulted ceiling and fills the area with natural light. An oversize masonry fireplace is flanked by a set of sliding glass doors opening to the deck. The U-shaped kitchen has great counter and shelf space. Pocket doors seclude it from the dining room and the laundry room at the back. Behind the laundry room is a bedroom with wall closet. It shares a bath with the master bedroom, which has a walk-in closet. A vaulted loft can serve as additional sleeping space.

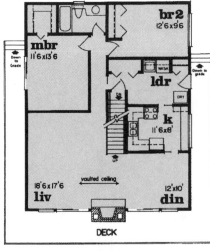

FIRST FLOOR

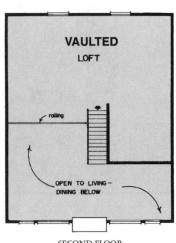

SECOND FLOOR

ORDER BLUEPRINTS 24 HOURS, 7 DAYS A WEEK, AT 1-800-521-6797

An expansive wall of glass, rising to the roof's peak, adds architectural interest and gives the living room of this home a spectacular view. The living room also boasts a vaulted ceiling, an oversized masonry fireplace, and access to a deck with a wonderful spa tub. The dining room is nearby, directly across from the galley-style kitchen. Two bedrooms sit to the rear of the plan and share a full bath. The second-level master suite caters to comfort with a walk-in closet, spa tub, and separate shower. Note how the open-rail staircase winds to the gallery on the second floor and overlooks the living room below.

plan # HPK0200080

STYLE: VACATION
MAIN LEVEL: 552 SQ. FT.
LOWER LEVEL: 1,070 SQ. FT.
TOTAL: 1,622 SQ. FT.
BEDROOMS: 3
BATHROOMS: 2
DEPTH: 40' - 0"
FOUNDATION: BASEMENT

SEARCH ONLINE @ EPLANS.COM

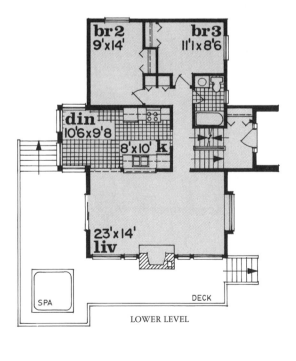

br2 9'x14'
br3 11'1x8'6
din 10'6x9'8
8'x10' k
23'x14' liv
SPA
DECK

LOWER LEVEL

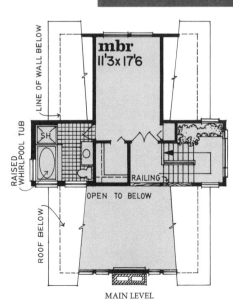

LINE OF WALL BELOW
mbr 11'3x17'6
RAISED WHIRLPOOL TUB
SH
RAILING
OPEN TO BELOW
ROOF BELOW

MAIN LEVEL

THE PERFECT GETAWAY
RUSTIC COTTAGES AND VACATION HOMES

plan # HPK0200081

STYLE: VACATION
MAIN LEVEL: 787 SQ. FT.
LOWER LEVEL: 787 SQ. FT.
TOTAL: 1,574 SQ. FT.
BEDROOMS: 3
BATHROOMS: 2
DEPTH: 24' - 4"
FOUNDATION: BASEMENT

SEARCH ONLINE @ EPLANS.COM

This chalet-style design offers wonderful views for vacations and plenty of comfort for year-round living. The main level includes complete living quarters, with one bedroom, a full bath, and an open living and dining area, which accesses the front. Sliding glass doors lead from the eat-in kitchen to the wraparound deck, and a V-shaped fireplace warms the entire area. The lower level provides two additional bedrooms, a full bath with laundry facilities, and a family room with outdoor access.

MAIN LEVEL

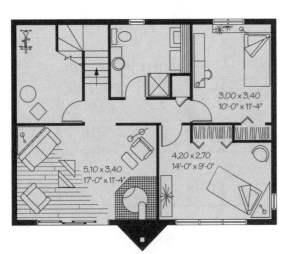

LOWER LEVEL

ORDER BLUEPRINTS 24 HOURS, 7 DAYS A WEEK, AT 1-800-521-6797

THE PERFECT GETAWAY
RUSTIC COTTAGES AND VACATION HOMES

This mountain-top chalet takes advantage of views with tall floor-to-ceiling windows. A central fireplace runs straight up from the lower-level family room to the living/dining room as a visual statement of warmth. A large efficient kitchen, living room, dining area, bedroom, and full bath complete the main level. Downstairs, two bedrooms share a full bath and a laundry room. A family room accesses the patio through sliding glass doors.

plan# HPK0200082

STYLE: HILLSIDE
MAIN LEVEL: 787 SQ. FT.
LOWER LEVEL: 787 SQ. FT.
TOTAL: 1,574 SQ. FT.
BEDROOMS: 3
BATHROOMS: 2
DEPTH: 24' - 4"
FOUNDATION: BASEMENT

SEARCH ONLINE @ EPLANS.COM

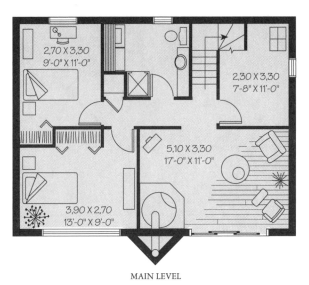

MAIN LEVEL

LOWER LEVEL

THE PERFECT GETAWAY
RUSTIC COTTAGES AND VACATION HOMES

plan# HPK0200083

STYLE: VACATION
FIRST FLOOR: 974 SQ. FT.
SECOND FLOOR: 322 SQ. FT.
TOTAL: 1,296 SQ. FT.
BEDROOMS: 3
BATHROOMS: 1
WIDTH: 36' - 0"
DEPTH: 45' - 3"
FOUNDATION: CRAWLSPACE

SEARCH ONLINE @ EPLANS.COM

With a striking roofline and impressive stone chimney, this cottage is the essence of rustic design. Walls of glass fill the living/dining room and the kitchen with sunlight. A corner hearth serves both the living and dining areas and allows for a built-in barbecue on the wide wrapping deck. The U-shaped kitchen has a built-in breakfast bar. Two bedrooms sit to the rear of the home and share the use of a full bath. A third bedroom on the second level has a balcony overlook to the living area below. Note the extra-large storage areas on the second floor.

SECOND FLOOR

FIRST FLOOR

Stone and siding work together to complement this cozy design. The vaulted living and dining rooms, with exposed beam ceilings, are open to the loft above. A spacious wood storage area is found off the living room to feed the warm hearth inside. The kitchen features a pass-through counter to the dining area and leads to a laundry room with work bench. The master suite is on the first floor and has a private patio and bath. An additional half-bath is located in the main hall. The second floor holds a family room with desk and two family bedrooms with shared bath.

plan⊕# HPK0200084

STYLE: VACATION
FIRST FLOOR: 1,036 SQ. FT.
SECOND FLOOR: 630 SQ. FT.
TOTAL: 1,666 SQ. FT.
BEDROOMS: 3
BATHROOMS: 2½
WIDTH: 45' - 6"
DEPTH: 44' - 0"
FOUNDATION: CRAWLSPACE

SEARCH ONLINE @ EPLANS.COM

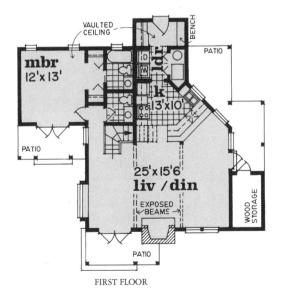

FIRST FLOOR

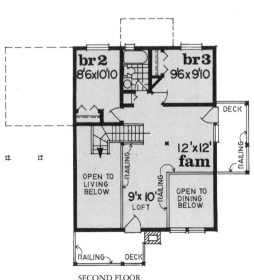

SECOND FLOOR

THE PERFECT GETAWAY
RUSTIC COTTAGES AND VACATION HOMES

plan# HPK0200085

STYLE: VACATION
FIRST FLOOR: 1,084 SQ. FT.
SECOND FLOOR: 343 SQ. FT.
TOTAL: 1,427 SQ. FT.
BEDROOMS: 3
BATHROOMS: 2
WIDTH: 37' - 0"
DEPTH: 36' - 0"
FOUNDATION: CRAWLSPACE

SEARCH ONLINE @ EPLANS.COM

Vertical siding and a wide deck grace the exterior of this plan. French doors open to the living/dining room. Extra-high vaulted ceilings and a wall of windows make the living/dining room a comfortable gathering area. This area is warmed by a fireplace and opens to the U-shaped kitchen. A laundry room sits just beyond. Access the rear deck through the kitchen. Bedrooms 2 and 3 share a full bath. The floor plan features a secluded second-floor master suite with a private bath and walk-in closet.

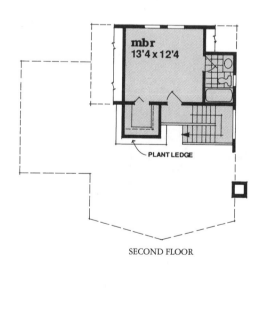

mbr
13'4 x 12'4

PLANT LEDGE

SECOND FLOOR

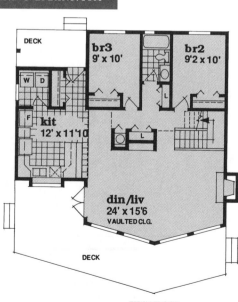

DECK

br3
9' x 10'

br2
9'2 x 10'

W D

F

kit
12' x 11'10

din/liv
24' x 15'6
VAULTED CLG.

DECK

FIRST FLOOR

ORDER BLUEPRINTS 24 HOURS, 7 DAYS A WEEK, AT 1-800-521-6797

THE PERFECT GETAWAY
RUSTIC COTTAGES AND VACATION HOMES

An expansive window wall across the great room of this home adds a spectacular view and accentuates the high ceiling. The open kitchen shares an eating bar with the dining room and features a convenient "U" shape. Sliding glass doors in the dining room lead to the deck. Two family bedrooms sit to the back of the plan and share the use of a full bath. The master suite provides a walk-in closet and private bath. The loft on the upper level adds living or sleeping space.

plan # HPK0200086

STYLE: NW CONTEMPORARY
FIRST FLOOR: 1,375 SQ. FT.
SECOND FLOOR: 284 SQ. FT.
TOTAL: 1,659 SQ. FT.
BEDROOMS: 3
BATHROOMS: 2
WIDTH: 58' - 0"
DEPTH: 32' - 0"
FOUNDATION: CRAWLSPACE,
BASEMENT

SEARCH ONLINE @ EPLANS.COM

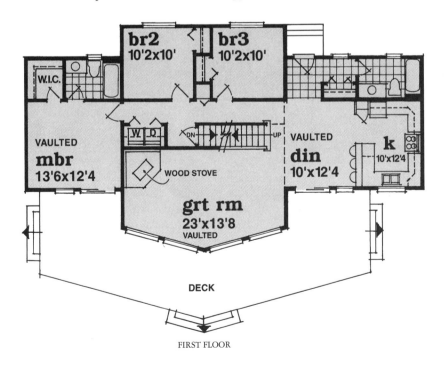

FIRST FLOOR

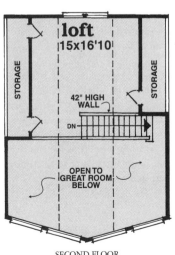

SECOND FLOOR

THE PERFECT GETAWAY
RUSTIC COTTAGES AND VACATION HOMES

plan# HPK0200087

STYLE: LAKESIDE
SQUARE FOOTAGE: 1,230
BEDROOMS: 3
BATHROOMS: 2
WIDTH: 33' - 0"
DEPTH: 30' - 0"
FOUNDATION: BASEMENT,
CRAWLSPACE

SEARCH ONLINE @ EPLANS.COM

This is a grand vacation or retirement home, designed for views and the outdoor lifestyle. The full-width deck complements the abundant windows in rooms facing its way. The living room is made for gathering with a vaulted ceiling, a fireplace, and full-height windows overlooking the deck. Open to this living space is the dining room with sliding glass doors to the outdoors and a pass-through counter to the U-shaped kitchen. Two family bedrooms sit in the middle of the plan. They share a full bath. The master suite features a private bath and deck views.

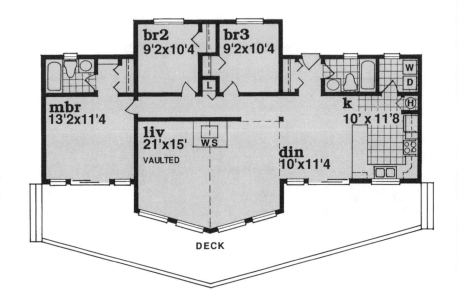

THE PERFECT GETAWAY

RUSTIC COTTAGES AND VACATION HOMES

plan# HPK0200088

STYLE: VACATION
FIRST FLOOR: 1,437 SQ. FT.
SECOND FLOOR: 1,635 SQ. FT.
TOTAL: 3,072 SQ. FT.
BEDROOMS: 4
BATHROOMS: 3
WIDTH: 62' - 0"
DEPTH: 36' - 0"
FOUNDATION: BASEMENT

SEARCH ONLINE @ EPLANS.COM

This beautiful chalet vacation home abounds with views of the outdoors and provides a grand deck, creating additional living space. With its entry on the lower level, you'll find two family bedrooms that share a full bath, an office/study, and a family room with a warming fireplace. There's an extra room here that could be a third family bedroom or perhaps a library or study. Upstairs, a great room with a cathedral ceiling shares a through-fireplace with the formal dining room. Conveniently nearby is the kitchen, which boasts an island work area/snack bar and an informal dining area. Also on this upper level is the master suite with its own private bath. Also on this floor, a fourth bedroom and another full bath would certainly accommodate weekend or overnight guests.

SECOND FLOOR

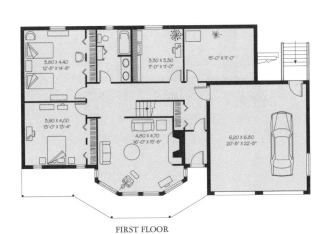

FIRST FLOOR

THE PERFECT GETAWAY
RUSTIC COTTAGES AND VACATION HOMES

plan# HPK0200089

STYLE: VACATION
FIRST FLOOR: 1,296 SQ. FT.
SECOND FLOOR: 396 SQ. FT.
TOTAL: 1,692 SQ. FT.
BEDROOMS: 3
BATHROOMS: 2
WIDTH: 55' - 6"
DEPTH: 33' - 0"
FOUNDATION: BASEMENT

SEARCH ONLINE @ EPLANS.COM

If your lot slopes to the front and enjoys a view in that direction, this may be the perfect plan for you. The prow front features a wall of windows extending a full two stories, to ensure a view from both the loft and the living room. The huge deck can be accessed from the dining room or the master bedroom and also shelters the lower-level entry. The master suite is on the main living level along with two family bedrooms. This main retreat features a private bath, and the family bedrooms share a full bath. A loft area provides additional sleeping space if you need it. The plan calls for the lower-level foyer and garage to be finished, with a complete unfinished basement available for future growth.

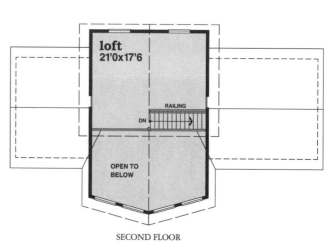

SECOND FLOOR

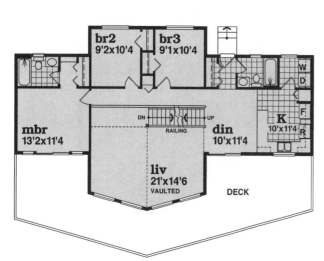

FIRST FLOOR

THE PERFECT GETAWAY
RUSTIC COTTAGES AND VACATION HOMES

This three-bedroom leisure home is perfect for the family that spends casual time out of doors. An expansive wall of glass gives a spectacular view to the great room and accentuates the high vaulted ceilings throughout the design. The great room is also warmed by a woodstove and is open to the dining room and L-shaped kitchen. A triangular snack bar graces the kitchen and provides space for casual meals. Bedrooms are split, with the master bedroom on the right side of the plan and family bedrooms on the left.

plan# HPK0200090

STYLE: VACATION
SQUARE FOOTAGE: 1,405
BEDROOMS: 3
BATHROOMS: 2
WIDTH: 62' - 0"
DEPTH: 29' - 0"
FOUNDATION: CRAWLSPACE, BASEMENT

SEARCH ONLINE @ EPLANS.COM

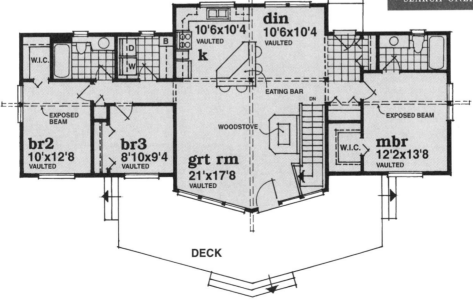

THE PERFECT GETAWAY
RUSTIC COTTAGES AND VACATION HOMES

© 1987 Donald A. Gardner Architects, Inc.

plan # HPK0200091

STYLE: NORTHWEST CONTEMPORARY
SQUARE FOOTAGE: 1,426
BEDROOMS: 3
BATHROOMS: 2½
WIDTH: 67' - 6"
DEPTH: 36' - 8"

SEARCH ONLINE @ EPLANS.COM

Rustic charm abounds in this amenity-filled, three-bedroom plan. From the central living area with its cathedral ceiling and fireplace to the sumptuous master suite, this plan has it all. Be sure to notice the large walk-in closet in the master bedroom, the pampering whirlpool tub, and the separate toilet compartment. Two other bedrooms have a connecting bath with a vanity for each. Note the screened porch with skylights, a grand place for eating and entertaining. The spacious rear deck has plenty of room for a hot tub.

REAR EXTERIOR

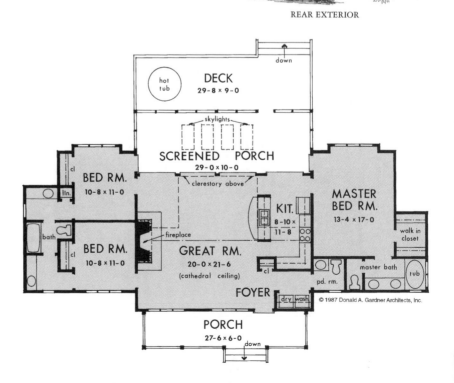

© 1987 Donald A. Gardner Architects, Inc.

THE PERFECT GETAWAY
RUSTIC COTTAGES AND VACATION HOMES

© 1987 Donald A. Gardner Architects, Inc.

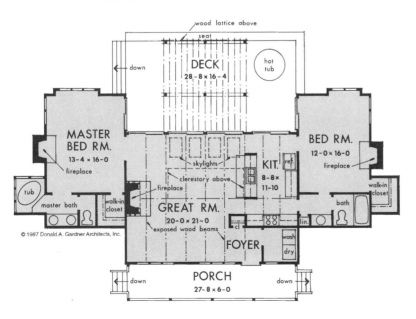

REAR EXTERIOR

plan# HPK0200092

STYLE: KEY WEST STYLE
SQUARE FOOTAGE: 1,299
BEDROOMS: 2
BATHROOMS: 2
WIDTH: 65' - 4"
DEPTH: 35' - 0"

SEARCH ONLINE @ EPLANS.COM

Though rustic in appearance, this two-bedroom plan provides all the features sought after in today's well-planned home. A large central area includes a great room, entrance foyer, and kitchen, with a serving and eating counter. Note the use of cathedral ceilings with exposed wood beams, skylights, clerestory windows, and a fireplace in this area. The master suite has an optional fireplace, a walk-in closet, and a whirlpool tub. The second bedroom also has an optional fireplace and a full bath. All rooms open to the rear deck, which supplies space for a hot tub.

wood lattice above
seat

DECK
28-8 × 16-4

hot tub

down

MASTER BED RM.
13-4 × 16-0
fireplace

skylights

clerestory above

fireplace

KIT.
8-8 × 11-10

ref.

BED RM.
12-0 × 16-0
fireplace

tub

master bath

walk-in closet

GREAT RM.
20-0 × 21-0
exposed wood beams

walk-in closet

bath

© 1987 Donald A. Gardner Architects, Inc.

cl.

lin.

FOYER

wash dry

PORCH
27-8 × 6-0

down

down

THE PERFECT GETAWAY
RUSTIC COTTAGES AND VACATION HOMES

plan# HPK0200093

STYLE: VACATION
SQUARE FOOTAGE: 2,019
BEDROOMS: 3
BATHROOMS: 2
WIDTH: 56' - 0"
DEPTH: 56' - 3"
FOUNDATION: CRAWLSPACE

SEARCH ONLINE @ EPLANS.COM

REAR EXTERIOR

This design takes inspiration from the casual fishing cabins of the Pacific Northwest and interprets it for modern livability. It offers three options for a main entrance. One door opens to a mud porch, where a small hall leads to a galley kitchen and the vaulted great room. Two French doors on the side porch open into a dining room with bay-window seating. Another porch entrance opens directly into the great room, which is centered around a massive stone fireplace and accented with a wall of windows. The secluded master bedroom features a bath with a clawfoot tub and twin pedestal sinks, as well as a separate shower and walk-in closet. Two more bedrooms share a bath. An unfinished loft looks over the great room.

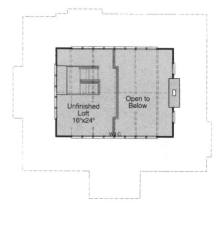

THE PERFECT GETAWAY
RUSTIC COTTAGES AND VACATION HOMES

R. DENT '99   © American Home Gallery, Ltd.

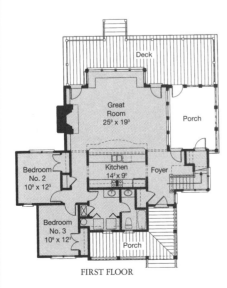

REAR EXTERIOR

plan# HPK0200094

STYLE: VACATION
FIRST FLOOR: 1,341 SQ. FT.
SECOND FLOOR: 598 SQ. FT.
TOTAL: 1,939 SQ. FT.
BEDROOMS: 3
BATHROOMS: 2
WIDTH: 50' - 3"
DEPTH: 46' - 3"
FOUNDATION: CRAWLSPACE

SEARCH ONLINE @ EPLANS.COM

Horizontal siding, plentiful windows, and a wraparound porch grace this comfortable home. The great room is aptly named, with a fireplace, built-in seating, and access to the rear deck. Meal preparation is a breeze with a galley kitchen designed for efficiency. A screened porch is available for sipping lemonade on warm summer afternoons. The first floor contains two bedrooms and a unique bath to serve family and guests. The second floor offers a private getaway with a master suite that supplies panoramic views from its adjoining sitting area. A master bath with His and Hers walk-in closets and a private deck completes the second floor.

Deck

Open
To
Below

Deck

Sitting
Area

Master
Bedroom
14³ x 14³

SECOND FLOOR

Deck

Great
Room
25⁸ x 19³

Porch

Bedroom
No. 2
10⁸ x 12³

Kitchen
14³ x 9⁹

Foyer

Bedroom
No. 3
10⁸ x 12³

Porch

FIRST FLOOR

© 1991 Donald A. Gardner Architects, Inc.

plan # HPK0200095

STYLE: KEY WEST STYLE
FIRST FLOOR: 1,002 SQ. FT.
SECOND FLOOR: 336 SQ. FT.
TOTAL: 1,338 SQ. FT.
BEDROOMS: 3
BATHROOMS: 2
WIDTH: 36' - 8"
DEPTH: 44' - 8"

SEARCH ONLINE @ EPLANS.COM

A mountain retreat, this rustic home features covered porches at the front and rear. Enjoy open living in the great room and kitchen/dining room combination. Here, a fireplace provides the focal point and a warm welcome that continues into the L-shaped island kitchen. A cathedral ceiling graces the great room and gives an open, inviting sense of space. Two bedrooms and a full bath on the first level are complemented by a master bedroom on the second floor. This suite includes a walk-in closet and deluxe bath. Attic storage is available on the second floor.

SECOND FLOOR

FIRST FLOOR

THE PERFECT GETAWAY
RUSTIC COTTAGES AND VACATION HOMES

© 1992 Donald A. Gardner Architects, Inc.

This economical, rustic, three-bedroom plan sports a relaxing country image with both front and back covered porches. The openness of the expansive great room to the kitchen/dining areas and the loft/study areas is reinforced with a shared cathedral ceiling for impressive space. The first floor provides two bedrooms, a full bath, and a utility area. The master suite upstairs offers a walk-in closet and a whirlpool tub.

plan # HPK0200096

STYLE: FARMHOUSE
FIRST FLOOR: 1,027 SQ. FT.
SECOND FLOOR: 580 SQ. FT.
TOTAL: 1,607 SQ. FT.
BEDROOMS: 3
BATHROOMS: 2
WIDTH: 37' - 4"
DEPTH: 44' - 8"

SEARCH ONLINE @ EPLANS.COM

PORCH
34-4 × 8-0

KIT./DINING
18-0 × 11-8

BED RM.
12-0 × 10-0

bath

loft above

cl

w/d

cl

GREAT RM.
17-4 × 16-4

fireplace

BED RM.
12-0 × 12-4

up

PORCH
34-4 × 8-0

© 1992 Donald A. Gardner Architects, Inc.

FIRST FLOOR

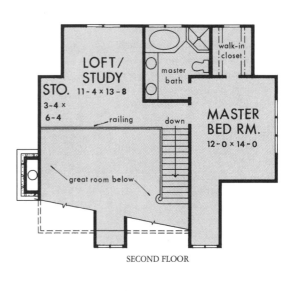

LOFT/
STUDY
11-4 × 13-8

STO.
3-4 ×
6-4

walk-in
closet

master
bath

railing

down

great room below

MASTER
BED RM.
12-0 × 14-0

SECOND FLOOR

THE PERFECT GETAWAY
RUSTIC COTTAGES AND VACATION HOMES

plan# HPK0200097

STYLE: CRAFTSMAN
SQUARE FOOTAGE: 1,643
BONUS SPACE: 290 SQ. FT.
BEDROOMS: 3
BATHROOMS: 2
WIDTH: 51' - 0"
DEPTH: 57' - 0"
FOUNDATION: CRAWLSPACE

SEARCH ONLINE @ EPLANS.COM

This fine Craftsman bungalow will look good in any neighborhood and will surely be a family favorite. Entertaining will be a breeze with the open living and dining area, which is highlighted by a fireplace and access to the rear patio. The L-shaped kitchen offers a large island and an adjacent nook for casual times. Split bedrooms ensure privacy, with the sumptuous master suite on the right side of the home and two family bedrooms on the left, sharing a full bath. The master suite is designed with amenities, including a walk-in closet and a separate tub and shower. The unfinished bonus space is available for future use as a home office, a playroom for kids, a media room, or a guest suite.

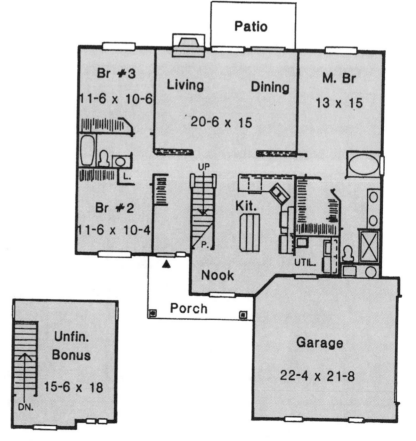

THE PERFECT GETAWAY
RUSTIC COTTAGES AND VACATION HOMES

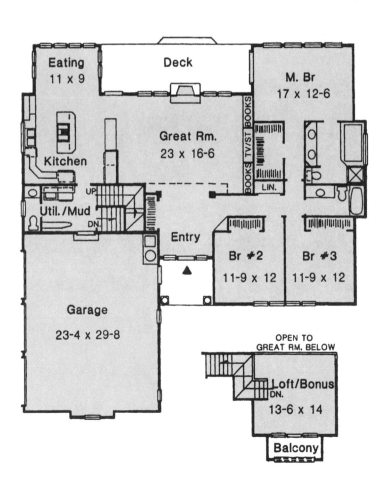

plan# HPK0200098

STYLE: SHINGLE
SQUARE FOOTAGE: 1,941
BONUS SPACE: 200 SQ. FT.
BEDROOMS: 3
BATHROOMS: 2½
WIDTH: 60' - 0"
DEPTH: 62' - 0"
FOUNDATION: BASEMENT,
CRAWLSPACE

SEARCH ONLINE @ EPLANS.COM

A trio of gables adorn this fine three-bed-room bungalow. Accented by shingles and siding with a welcoming porch, this fine home will dress up any neighborhood. Inside, the efficient kitchen easily serves the sunny nook as well as the family room. Patio access from the family room expands the space for tons of outdoor fun. A separate living room is available for formal gatherings. Upstairs, two family bedrooms share a full hall bath; the master bedroom suite features a walk-in closet and a private bath. A large bonus room on this level is perfect for a playroom, study, or fourth bedroom. The two-car garage has an option for a third-car bay.

THE PERFECT GETAWAY
RUSTIC COTTAGES AND VACATION HOMES

plan# HPK0200099

STYLE: CRAFTSMAN
SQUARE FOOTAGE: 1,922
BEDROOMS: 3
BATHROOMS: 2½
WIDTH: 79' - 3"
DEPTH: 40' - 0"
FOUNDATION: SLAB

SEARCH ONLINE @ EPLANS.COM

In the Craftsman tradition, this one-story home is enhanced by rubblework masonry and multipane windows. The covered porch leads into the entry, flanked by the living room and formal dining room. The hearth-warmed family room enjoys views to the rear screened porch. The island kitchen provides plenty of counter space and close proximity to the breakfast nook. All bedrooms reside on the left side of the plan. The master bedroom boasts a private covered patio and lavish full bath, and two family bedrooms share a full bath. A unique shop area attached to the two-car garage completes the plan.

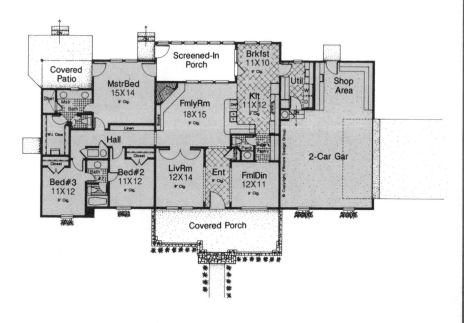

©1999 Donald A. Gardner, Inc.

REAR EXTERIOR

SECOND FLOOR

FIRST FLOOR

©1999 Donald A. Gardner, Inc.

plan⊕ HPK0200100

STYLE: TRADITIONAL
FIRST FLOOR: 2,908 SQ. FT.
SECOND FLOOR: 1,021 SQ. FT.
TOTAL: 3,929 SQ. FT.
BONUS SPACE: 328 SQ. FT.
BEDROOMS: 5
BATHROOMS: 4
WIDTH: 85' - 4"
DEPTH: 70' - 4"

SEARCH ONLINE @ EPLANS.COM

Siding and stone embellish the exterior of this five-bedroom traditional estate for an exciting, yet stately appearance. A two-story foyer creates an impressive entry. An equally impressive two-story great room features a fireplace, built-ins, and back-porch access. The first-floor master suite enjoys an elegant tray ceiling, back-porch access, and a lavish bath with all the amenities, including an enormous walk-in closet. Down the hall, a second first-floor bedroom easily converts to a study. The island kitchen easily serves the dining and breakfast rooms. A fireplace warms the casual family room. The breakfast room accesses the screened porch. Three additional bedrooms are on the second floor. The bonus room above the garage is great for attic storage, a home office, or a guest suite.

THE PERFECT GETAWAY
RUSTIC COTTAGES AND VACATION HOMES

plan # HPK0200101

STYLE: CRAFTSMAN
FIRST FLOOR: 2,078 SQ. FT.
SECOND FLOOR: 823 SQ. FT.
TOTAL: 2,901 SQ. FT.
BEDROOMS: 3
BATHROOMS: 2½
WIDTH: 88' - 5"
DEPTH: 58' - 3"
FOUNDATION: BASEMENT

SEARCH ONLINE @ EPLANS.COM

The strong impact of its exterior design will make this home look good in the country or the suburbs. Upon entering, guests are greeted with the expansive great room's cathedral ceiling and cozy fireplace. The kitchen has a snack-counter island with a breakfast nook that opens to a deck. Located on the first floor for privacy, the master suite contains plenty of windows, two walk-in closets, and a whirlpool tub with views out a bay window. The immaculate second floor overlooks the great room and entryway. A lounge area is flanked by Bedrooms 2 and 3. A full bath with dual vanities completes the plan.

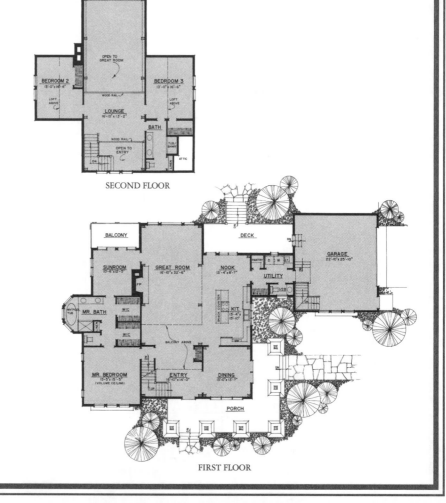

SECOND FLOOR

FIRST FLOOR

ORDER BLUEPRINTS 24 HOURS, 7 DAYS A WEEK, AT 1-800-521-6797

THE PERFECT GETAWAY
RUSTIC COTTAGES AND VACATION HOMES

plan# HPK0200102

STYLE: BUNGALOW
FIRST FLOOR: 1,855 SQ. FT.
SECOND FLOOR: 901 SQ. FT.
TOTAL: 2,756 SQ. FT.
BEDROOMS: 3
BATHROOMS: 3½
WIDTH: 66' - 0"
DEPTH: 50' - 0"
FOUNDATION: BASEMENT

SEARCH ONLINE @ EPLANS.COM

This luxurious vacation cabin is the perfect rustic paradise, whether set by a lake or in a mountain scene. The wraparound entry porch is friendly and inviting. Double doors open to the foyer, which is flanked on either side by the study with built-in cabinetry and the formal dining room. The octagonal great room features a multifaceted vaulted ceiling, fireplace, built-in entertainment center, and three sets of double doors leading to a vaulted lanai. The gourmet island kitchen is brightened by a bay window and a pass-through to the lanai.

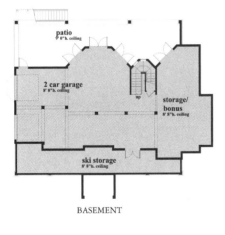

BASEMENT

FIRST FLOOR

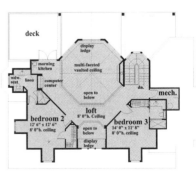

SECOND FLOOR

THE PERFECT GETAWAY
RUSTIC COTTAGES AND VACATION HOMES

plan # HPK0200103

STYLE: CRAFTSMAN
FIRST FLOOR: 1,383 SQ. FT.
SECOND FLOOR: 595 SQ. FT.
TOTAL: 1,978 SQ. FT.
BEDROOMS: 3
BATHROOMS: 2
WIDTH: 48' - 0"
DEPTH: 48' - 8"
FOUNDATION: BASEMENT

SEARCH ONLINE @ EPLANS.COM

The stone facade and woodwork detail give this home a Craftsman appeal. The foyer opens to a staircase up to the vaulted great room, which features a fireplace flanked by built-ins and French-door access to the rear covered porch. The open dining room with a tray ceiling offers convenience to the spacious kitchen. Two family bedrooms share a bath and enjoy private porches. An overlook to the great room below is a perfect introduction to the master suite. The second level spreads out the luxury of the master suite with a spacious walk-in closet, a private porch, and a glorious master bath with a garden tub, dual vanities, and a compartmented toilet.

REAR EXTERIOR

SECOND FLOOR

FIRST FLOOR

BASEMENT

This charming rustic home has a lot to offer including five bedrooms. The formal dining room and parlor flank the foyer, which opens to the gallery with its grand, split-ascending staircase announcing the dazzling, two-story family room. On the left is the private master suite and on the right is the island kitchen, laundry and sunny breakfast nook. The second floor holds four family bedrooms and a full bath.

plan# HPK0200104

STYLE: CRAFTSMAN
FIRST FLOOR: 1,554 SQ. FT.
SECOND FLOOR: 1,075 SQ. FT.
TOTAL: 2,629 SQ. FT.
BEDROOMS: 5
BATHROOMS: 2½
WIDTH: 68' - 0"
DEPTH: 54' - 0"
FOUNDATION: CRAWLSPACE, BASEMENT

SEARCH ONLINE @ EPLANS.COM

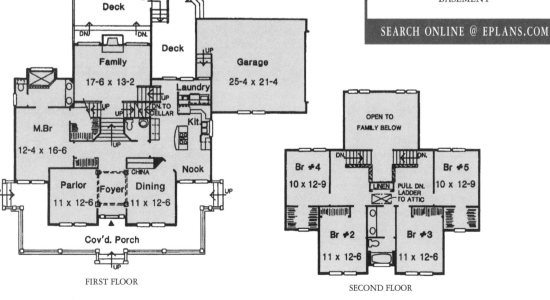

FIRST FLOOR

SECOND FLOOR

THE PERFECT GETAWAY
RUSTIC COTTAGES AND VACATION HOMES

plan# HPK0200105

STYLE: BUNGALOW
FIRST FLOOR: 1,292 SQ. FT.
SECOND FLOOR: 423 SQ. FT.
TOTAL: 1,715 SQ. FT.
BEDROOMS: 3
BATHROOMS: 2½
WIDTH: 40' - 0"
DEPTH: 59' - 8"

SEARCH ONLINE @ EPLANS.COM

This narrow-lot plan is highlighted by an entrance with a barrel-vaulted ceiling and flanking detailed pillars. The great room and dining room share a vaulted ceiling to the second level. A spacious kitchen boasts an island and convenient breakfast area leading to the deck. The master bedroom on the main level has a large walk-in closet and complete master bath including a double-bowl vanity, whirlpool tub, separate shower, and linen storage. The second level accommodates two bedrooms, a full bath, a balcony, and attic storage.

FIRST FLOOR

SECOND FLOOR

© 1998 Donald A. Gardner Architects, Inc.

REAR EXTERIOR

plan # HPK0200106

STYLE: CRAFTSMAN
FIRST FLOOR: 1,896 SQ. FT.
SECOND FLOOR: 692 SQ. FT.
TOTAL: 2,588 SQ. FT.
BEDROOMS: 3
BATHROOMS: 2½
WIDTH: 60' - 0"
DEPTH: 84' - 10"

SEARCH ONLINE @ EPLANS.COM

FIRST FLOOR

SECOND FLOOR

This fine three-bedroom home is full of amenities and will surely be a family favorite! A covered porch leads into the great room/dining room. Here, a fireplace reigns at one end, casting its glow throughout the room. A private study is tucked away, perfect for a home office or computer study. The master bedroom suite offers a bayed sitting area, large walk-in closet, and pampering bath. With plenty of counter and cabinet space and an adjacent breakfast area, the kitchen will be a favorite gathering place for casual mealtimes. The family sleeping zone is upstairs and includes two bedrooms, a full bath, a loft/study area, and a huge storage room.

THE PERFECT GETAWAY
RUSTIC COTTAGES AND VACATION HOMES

A bungalow-style plan, this home is enhanced with clerestory and multipane windows, unique pillars, and horizontal siding. Covered porches grace both the front and rear of this inviting home. Two doors access the spacious living room, where a fireplace heats up the space. The dining room adjoins the kitchen, which accesses the rear covered porch. The right side of the plan is devoted to sleeping quarters: a master suite, with a private full bath, and two additional bedrooms, complete with walk-in closets.

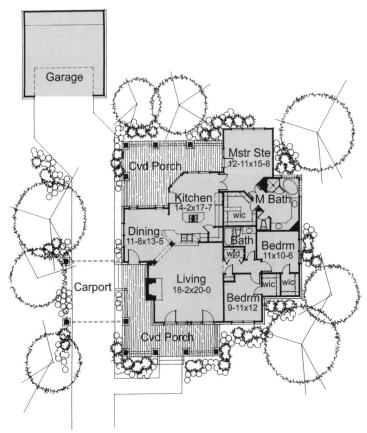

REAR EXTERIOR

SECOND FLOOR

plan # HPK0200108

STYLE: CRAFTSMAN
FIRST FLOOR: 1,836 SQ. FT.
SECOND FLOOR: 600 SQ. FT.
TOTAL: 2,436 SQ. FT.
BEDROOMS: 3
BATHROOMS: 2½
WIDTH: 86' - 7"
DEPTH: 54' - 0"
FOUNDATION: BASEMENT

SEARCH ONLINE @ EPLANS.COM

Interesting rooflines, a porte cochere, front and rear covered porches, and an angled entry are just the beginning of this bungalow design. The great room welcomes all with its fireplace and windowed views. The efficient kitchen includes access to the formal dining room, a breakfast nook, and a snack bar. An impressive master bedroom has French doors that open to a small entry area that could be used for a study, nursery, or sitting room. Two bedrooms on the upper level share a full bath and a study loft.

FIRST FLOOR

THE PERFECT GETAWAY
RUSTIC COTTAGES AND VACATION HOMES

plan# HPK0200109

STYLE: VACATION
FIRST FLOOR: 1,022 SQ. FT.
SECOND FLOOR: 551 SQ. FT.
TOTAL: 1,573 SQ. FT.
BEDROOMS: 2
BATHROOMS: 2
WIDTH: 39' - 0"
DEPTH: 32' - 0"
FOUNDATION: CRAWLSPACE

SEARCH ONLINE @ EPLANS.COM

This quaint cottage works equally well in the mountains or by the lake. It's entry is sliding glass, which opens to a vaulted living room with a fireplace tucked into a wide windowed bay. The dining room has sliding glass access to the deck. The skylit kitchen features a greenhouse window over the sink and is just across from a handy laundry room. The master bedroom captures views through sliding glass doors and a triangular feature window. The second floor holds another bedroom, a full bath, and a loft area that could be used as a bedroom, if you choose.

SECOND FLOOR

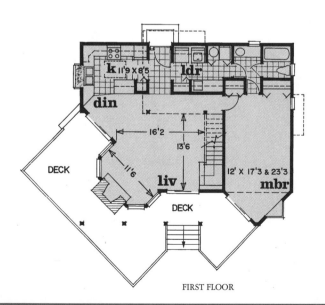

FIRST FLOOR

ORDER BLUEPRINTS 24 HOURS, 7 DAYS A WEEK, AT 1-800-521-6797

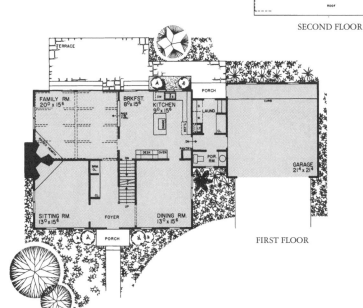

REAR EXTERIOR

SECOND FLOOR

plan# HPK0200110

STYLE: GAMBREL
FIRST FLOOR: 1,349 SQ. FT.
SECOND FLOOR: 836 SQ. FT.
TOTAL: 2,185 SQ. FT.
BEDROOMS: 3
BATHROOMS: 2½
WIDTH: 68' - 0"
DEPTH: 33' - 8"
FOUNDATION: BASEMENT

SEARCH ONLINE @ EPLANS.COM

FIRST FLOOR

This unusual bowed-roof Cape is based on a cottage from the 17th Century. The curved roof was also known as a ship's bottom built by the shipbuilders along the Atlantic coast. The house is a typical Cape, with two multi-pane windows on either side of the front door, all with full-length shutters. Inside is an outstanding plan with loads of livability. One raised-hearth fireplace warms the family room, and a second serves the sitting room. The kitchen area includes a work island, a pantry, and a breakfast nook with access to the terrace and a pass-through to the family room. The master suite boasts two walk-in closets and a private bath with an extended vanity.

THE EASTERN SEABOARD
STYLISH CAPE COD HOMES

plan # HPK0200111

STYLE: GAMBREL
FIRST FLOOR: 1,214 SQ. FT.
SECOND FLOOR: 1,097 SQ. FT.
TOTAL: 2,311 SQ. FT.
BEDROOMS: 4
BATHROOMS: 2½
WIDTH: 70' - 0"
DEPTH: 28' - 0"
FOUNDATION: BASEMENT

SEARCH ONLINE @ EPLANS.COM

The gambrel roof, vertical siding, and a hayloft door on the garage are inspired by Colonial cottages still popular in New England. The contemporary interior makes good use of the available space and retains an Early American flavor through such details as exposed beams in the family room, two fireplaces (one with a wood box), corner china cabinets, and decorative moldings and chair rails. The formal living and dining rooms are placed together for easy entertaining and for easy access from the U-shaped kitchen. A sliding door can be closed to keep out kitchen sounds when the meal is in progress. A sunny breakfast nook provides a cozy corner for informal dining. The second floor holds four bedrooms, including a master suite with a dressing room and a private bath.

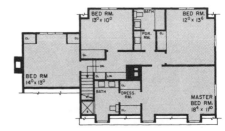

SECOND FLOOR

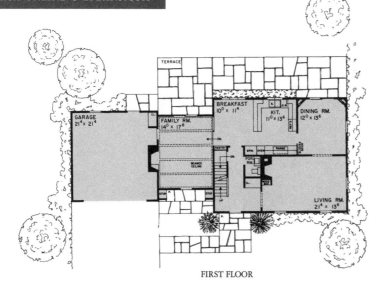

FIRST FLOOR

THE EASTERN SEABOARD
STYLISH CAPE COD HOMES

A gambrel roof provides volume and authenticity to this charming Cape Cod reproduction. Dormers front and rear pierce the roof to allow in plenty of natural light. The shutter-trimmed front door opens to a central foyer that leads to all areas of the house. Family and guests will all delight in the massive corner fireplace in the living room. A beamed ceiling contributes to the rustic atmosphere. Mealtime options include a dining room, breakfast room, and snack bar. The U-shaped kitchen easily serves them all. With both a covered porch and a patio, outdoor dining is another possibility. A front study has built-in bookshelves and would make a fine home office. Upstairs, three bedrooms include a master suite with a dressing room and twin vanities.

plan# HPK0200112

STYLE: CAPE COD
FIRST FLOOR: 1,122 SQ. FT.
SECOND FLOOR: 884 SQ. FT.
TOTAL: 2,006 SQ. FT.
BEDROOMS: 3
BATHROOMS: 2½
WIDTH: 53' - 8"
DEPTH: 39' - 4"
FOUNDATION: BASEMENT

SEARCH ONLINE @ EPLANS.COM

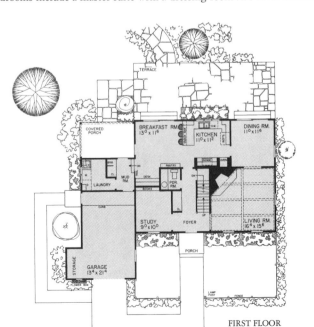

FIRST FLOOR

SECOND FLOOR

THE EASTERN SEABOARD
STYLISH CAPE COD HOMES

plan# HPK0200113

STYLE: CAPE COD
FIRST FLOOR: 1,234 SQ. FT.
SECOND FLOOR: 458 SQ. FT.
TOTAL: 1,692 SQ. FT.
BONUS SPACE: 236 SQ. FT.
BEDROOMS: 3
BATHROOMS: 2½
WIDTH: 48' - 6"
DEPTH: 42' - 4"
FOUNDATION: SLAB

SEARCH ONLINE @ EPLANS.COM

With New England charm, this early American Cape Cod home is a quaint haven for any family. Enter from the porch to the foyer, which opens to the dining area and great room. The great room is illuminated by a wall of windows and features a fireplace with two built-in niches on either side. An efficient kitchen is brightened by the morning room, which accesses an outdoor patio. The opposite side of the home is dedicated to the master suite, which includes a vaulted master bath and a spacious walk-in closet. A two-car garage completes this level. Two secondary bedrooms reside upstairs and share a full hall bath. An optional bonus room can be used as a fourth bedroom, a playroom, or a home office.

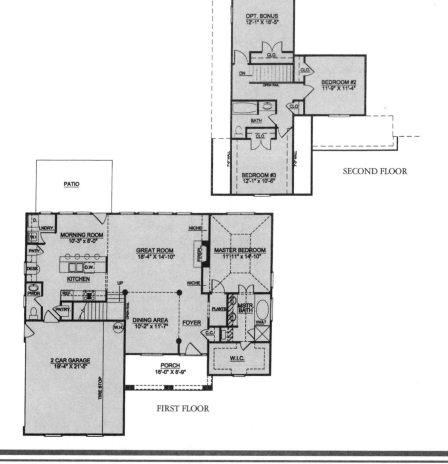

SECOND FLOOR

FIRST FLOOR

ORDER BLUEPRINTS 24 HOURS, 7 DAYS A WEEK, AT 1-800-521-6797

THE EASTERN SEABOARD
STYLISH CAPE COD HOMES

A barn-like facade gives this home plenty of charm and encourages relaxation. Imagine, five rooms for sleeping! A complete master bedroom suite, which includes a walk-in closet and a dressing area, plus three bedrooms and a bunk room. Three full baths, one on the first floor and two upstairs. The living room will enjoy easy access to a large deck through a wall of sliding glass doors, plus a fireplace. The dining room is conveniently located between the living area and the efficient kitchen which has a pantry and nearby laundry/utility room.

plan# HPK0200114

STYLE: GAMBREL
FIRST FLOOR: 1,160 SQ. FT.
SECOND FLOOR: 828 SQ. FT.
TOTAL: 1,988 SQ. FT.
BEDROOMS: 5
BATHROOMS: 3
WIDTH: 44' - 0"
DEPTH: 30' - 0"
FOUNDATION: CRAWLSPACE

SEARCH ONLINE @ EPLANS.COM

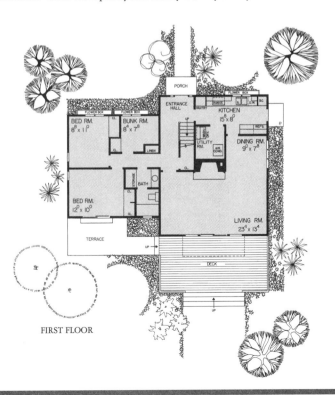

FIRST FLOOR

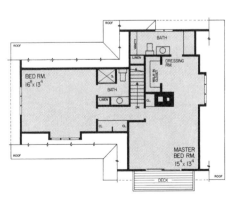

SECOND FLOOR

THE EASTERN SEABOARD
STYLISH CAPE COD HOMES

plan# HPK0200115

STYLE: CAPE COD
FIRST FLOOR: 1,296 SQ. FT.
SECOND FLOOR: 468 SQ. FT.
TOTAL: 1,764 SQ. FT.
BONUS SPACE: 169 SQ. FT.
BEDROOMS: 3
BATHROOMS: 2½
WIDTH: 49' - 0"
DEPTH: 46' - 0"
FOUNDATION: SLAB

SEARCH ONLINE @ EPLANS.COM

This tidy Southern cottage design opens with a covered front porch that protects the entry and adds a touch of down-home flavor. A central foyer is defined by columns that separate it from the formal dining room and the vaulted grand salon. Note the fireplace in the vaulted great room and the snack bar, which it shares with the kitchen. The master suite on the first floor features a vaulted ceiling and a bath with a separate tub and shower. Two family bedrooms on the second floor share a full bath. One of these bedrooms has a dormer window. Bonus space can be developed later to include a home office or an additional bedroom.

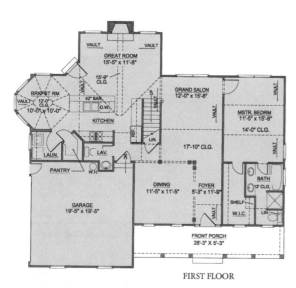

FIRST FLOOR

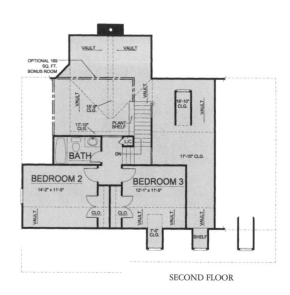

SECOND FLOOR

ORDER BLUEPRINTS 24 HOURS, 7 DAYS A WEEK, AT 1-800-521-6797

THE EASTERN SEABOARD
STYLISH CAPE COD HOMES

plan # HPK0200116

STYLE: COUNTRY COTTAGE
SQUARE FOOTAGE: 1,792
BONUS SPACE: 255 SQ. FT.
BEDROOMS: 3
BATHROOMS: 2
WIDTH: 50' - 0"
DEPTH: 62' - 6"
FOUNDATION: CRAWLSPACE, BASEMENT

SEARCH ONLINE @ EPLANS.COM

The country charm of this Cape Cod-style home belies the elegance inside. The beautiful foyer, accented by columns that define the formal dining room, leads to the family room. Here, the vaulted space is warm and cozy, courtesy of an extended-hearth fireplace. The kitchen is open and welcoming with angled counters that offer plenty of workspace. The laundry is conveniently located near the garage entrance. In the master suite, the star is the vaulted compartmented bath. Two additional bedrooms, both with ample closets, complete the plan. An optional upstairs addition includes a fourth bedroom and a full bath.

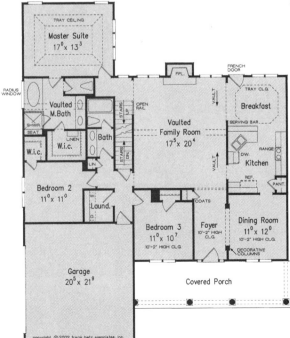

THE EASTERN SEABOARD
STYLISH CAPE COD HOMES

© 1997 Donald A. Gardner Architects, Inc.

plan # HPK0200117

STYLE: COUNTRY COTTAGE
SQUARE FOOTAGE: 2,349
BONUS SPACE: 435 SQ. FT.
BEDROOMS: 4
BATHROOMS: 3
WIDTH: 83' - 2"
DEPTH: 56' - 4"

SEARCH ONLINE @ EPLANS.COM

This plan's wide front porch says "welcome home." Inside, its comfortable design encourages relaxation. A center dormer lights the foyer, as columns punctuate the entry to the dining room and the great room. The spacious kitchen offers an angled countertop and is open to the breakfast bay. A roomy utility area is nearby. Tray ceilings add elegance to the dining room and master bedroom. A possible second master suite is located opposite and features an optional arrangement for wheelchair accessibility. Two additional bedrooms share a third full bath that includes a linen closet.

REAR EXTERIOR

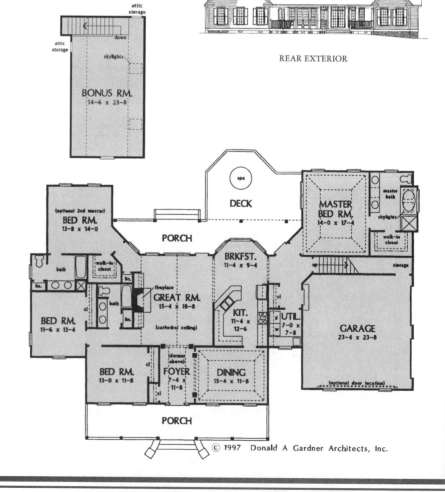

ORDER BLUEPRINTS 24 HOURS, 7 DAYS A WEEK, AT 1-800-521-6797

THE EASTERN SEABOARD
STYLISH CAPE COD HOMES

REAR EXTERIOR

plan# HPK0200118

STYLE: COLONIAL
SQUARE FOOTAGE: 1,781
BEDROOMS: 3
BATHROOMS: 2½
WIDTH: 87' - 4"
DEPTH: 42' - 8"
FOUNDATION: BASEMENT

SEARCH ONLINE @ EPLANS.COM

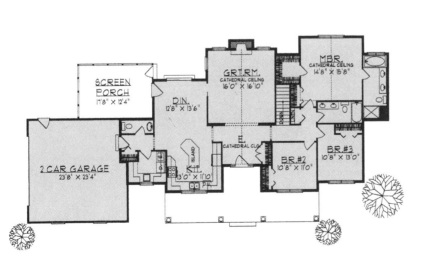

Three charming dormers over an arched entry are prelude to the convenient design inside. The entry contains a cathedral ceiling and opens to a great room, which also features a cathedral ceiling. The U-shaped kitchen has an island and connects with a spacious dining area. A screened porch opens just off the dining room. The master suite and two family bedrooms inhabit the right wing of the home. The master bath holds dual sinks and a separate tub and shower.

THE EASTERN SEABOARD
STYLISH CAPE COD HOMES

plan# HPK0200119

STYLE: CAPE COD
FIRST FLOOR: 1,632 SQ. FT.
SECOND FLOOR: 980 SQ. FT.
TOTAL: 2,612 SQ. FT.
BEDROOMS: 3
BATHROOMS: 2½ + ½
WIDTH: 80' - 0"
DEPTH: 35' - 4"
FOUNDATION: BASEMENT

SEARCH ONLINE @ EPLANS.COM

This delightful Cape Cod home offers three bedrooms and the charm of the colonial East Coast. The entry is flanked by the formal dining room and a spacious living room, which enjoys a warming fireplace and generous views to the outdoors. A second fireplace is found in the family room, which opens to the backyard. The sunny kitchen and nook are situated at the front of the home, which is ideal in regards to feng shui design. The den at the back converts easily to a guest room with a full bath near by.

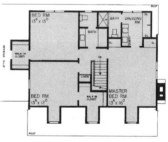

SECOND FLOOR

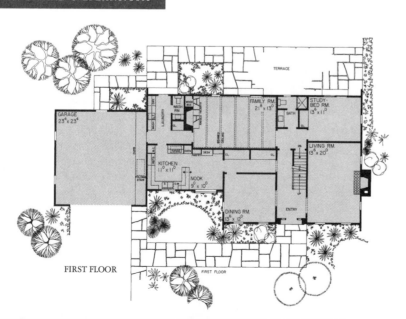

FIRST FLOOR

ORDER BLUEPRINTS 24 HOURS, 7 DAYS A WEEK, AT 1-800-521-6797

THE EASTERN SEABOARD
STYLISH CAPE COD HOMES

Another picturesque facade right from the pages of our colonial heritage. The first floor features many amenities. The entrance hall is flanked on the left by a living room with fireplace and on the right by a bedroom or study— your choice. Straight ahead, enter the kitchen and adjacent nook for informal dining. For more formal occasions, serve a meal in the back dining room, with a wide window view of the outside terrace. The family room is cozy with a beamed ceiling and its own fireplace. Upstairs, find the sleeping quarters away from the noisy living areas. Two bedrooms share a bath and the master bedroom will please with built-in desk, bookshelf, dressing room, closets, and bath.

plan# HPK0200120

STYLE: CAPE COD
FIRST FLOOR: 1,616 SQ. FT.
SECOND FLOOR: 993 SQ. FT.
TOTAL: 2,609 SQ. FT.
BEDROOMS: 3
BATHROOMS: 3
WIDTH: 84' - 0"
DEPTH: 40' - 0"
FOUNDATION: BASEMENT

SEARCH ONLINE @ EPLANS.COM

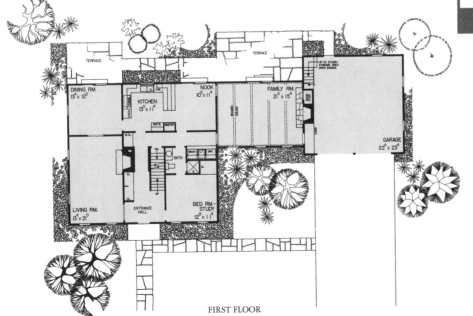

FIRST FLOOR

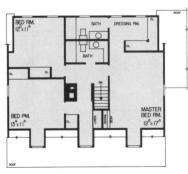

SECOND FLOOR

THE EASTERN SEABOARD
STYLISH CAPE COD HOMES

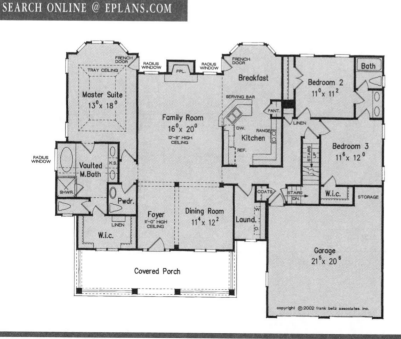

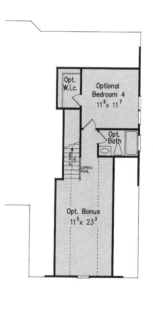

plan# HPK0200121

STYLE: COUNTRY COTTAGE
SQUARE FOOTAGE: 1,933
BONUS SPACE: 519 SQ. FT.
BEDROOMS: 3
BATHROOMS: 2½
WIDTH: 62' - 0"
DEPTH: 50' - 0"
FOUNDATION: CRAWLSPACE,
BASEMENT

SEARCH ONLINE @ EPLANS.COM

Traditional in every sense of the word, you can't go wrong with this charming country cottage. The foyer opens on the right to a columned dining room, and ahead to the family room. Here, a raised ceiling and bright radius windows expand the space, and a warming fireplace lends a cozy touch. A sunny bayed breakfast nook flows into the angled kitchen for easy casual meals. Down the hall, two bedrooms share a full bath, tucked behind the two-car garage to protect the bedrooms from street noise. The master suite is indulgent, pampering homeowners with a bayed sitting area, tray ceiling, vaulted spa bath, and an oversize walk-in closet. A fourth bedroom and bonus space are available to grow as your family does.

plan # HPK0200122

STYLE: CAPE COD
FIRST FLOOR: 996 SQ. FT.
SECOND FLOOR: 831 SQ. FT.
TOTAL: 1,827 SQ. FT.
BEDROOMS: 3
BATHROOMS: 2½
WIDTH: 61' - 0"
DEPTH: 35' - 6"
FOUNDATION: CRAWLSPACE,
BASEMENT

SEARCH ONLINE @ EPLANS.COM

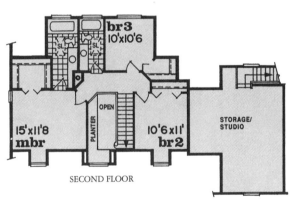

SECOND FLOOR

A richly gabled roofline defines this fine three-bedroom home. Double doors open to a wide foyer flanked by the formal living and dining rooms. The living room features a fireplace and double-door access to a screened porch. The country kitchen also accesses the screened porch and boasts a center work island, woodstove, greenhouse window, and space for a breakfast table. The two-car garage is reached via the service entrance through the laundry alcove. Three bedrooms on the second floor include a master suite with a walk-in closet and private skylit bath. Bedroom 3 also has a walk-in closet. Both family bedrooms share the use of a full hall bath that includes a skylight.

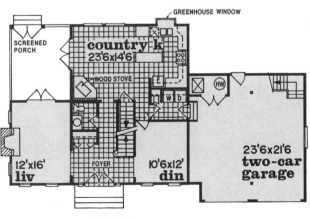

FIRST FLOOR

THE EASTERN SEABOARD
STYLISH CAPE COD HOMES

plan # HPK0200123

STYLE: CAPE COD
FIRST FLOOR: 2,145 SQ. FT.
SECOND FLOOR: 650 SQ. FT.
TOTAL: 2,795 SQ. FT.
BEDROOMS: 3
BATHROOMS: 2½
WIDTH: 73' - 0"
DEPTH: 76' - 8"
FOUNDATION: BASEMENT

SEARCH ONLINE @ EPLANS.COM

A brick facade, triple dormers, and a covered front porch create a striking presentation on this traditional home. Inside, the entry is flanked by a den and a formal dining room. The spacious great room is warmed by a fireplace straight ahead. A set of double doors from this room open to the rear wood deck—perfect for outdoor entertaining. The island kitchen resides between the breakfast nook/hearth room and a hallway with direct access to the laundry room and garage. The first-floor master bedroom features a large walk-in closet and a private bath. Two additional family bedrooms reside upstairs.

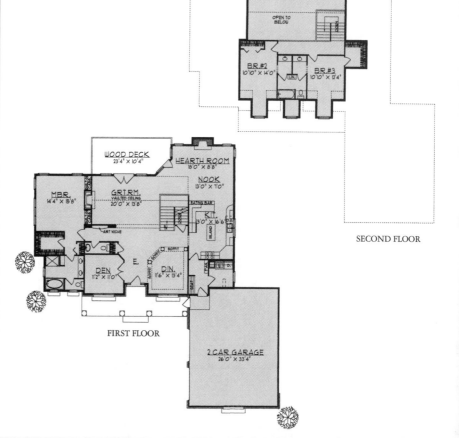

SECOND FLOOR

FIRST FLOOR

ORDER BLUEPRINTS 24 HOURS, 7 DAYS A WEEK, AT 1-800-521-6797

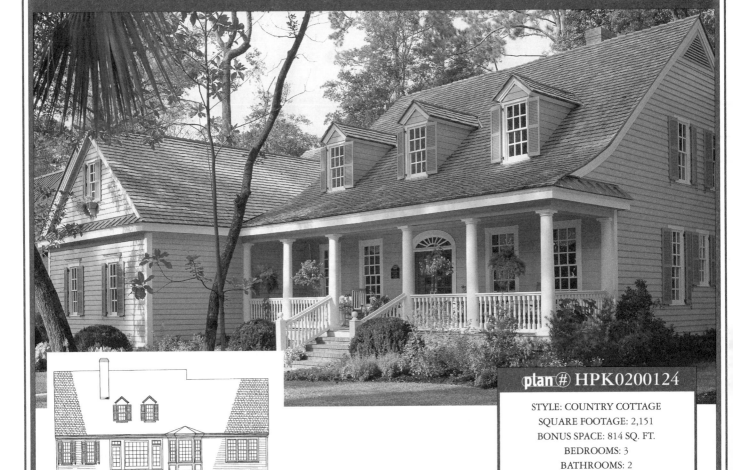

REAR EXTERIOR

SECOND FLOOR

FIRST FLOOR

plan# HPK0200124

STYLE: COUNTRY COTTAGE
SQUARE FOOTAGE: 2,151
BONUS SPACE: 814 SQ. FT.
BEDROOMS: 3
BATHROOMS: 2
WIDTH: 61' - 0"
DEPTH: 55' - 8"
FOUNDATION: CRAWLSPACE, BASEMENT

SEARCH ONLINE @ EPLANS.COM

Country flavor is well established on this fine three-bedroom home. The covered front porch welcomes friends and family alike to the foyer, where the formal dining room opens off to the left. The vaulted ceiling in the great room enhances the warmth of the fireplace and wall of windows. An efficient kitchen works well with the bayed breakfast area. The secluded master suite offers a walk-in closet and a lavish bath; on the other side of the home, two family bedrooms share a full bath. Upstairs, an optional fourth bedroom is available for guests or in-laws and provides access to a large recreation room.

THE EASTERN SEABOARD
STYLISH CAPE COD HOMES

plan⊕# HPK0200125

STYLE: CAPE COD
FIRST FLOOR: 1,634 SQ. FT.
SECOND FLOOR: 1,011 SQ. FT.
TOTAL: 2,645 SQ. FT.
BEDROOMS: 4
BATHROOMS: 3½
WIDTH: 80' - 0"
DEPTH: 32' - 0"
FOUNDATION: BASEMENT

SEARCH ONLINE @ EPLANS.COM

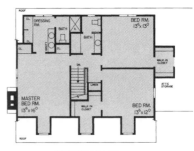

SECOND FLOOR

This Cape Cod-style house is based on those built by early colonial settlers along the Maryland coast. The main part of the exterior is symmetrical, with two small-paned and shuttered windows on either side of the simple front door and three dormers providing light to the second floor. The entry is flanked by a good-sized living room with a fireplace and a formal dining room. The addition of an ell makes possible the inclusion of a large family room, which provides space for a breakfast nook and the work areas of the home—a U-shaped kitchen, a laundry room, and a washroom. A first-floor study has access to a full bath, making it ideal as a guest suite. The second floor offers two bedrooms with walk-in closets and a master suite with a private bath.

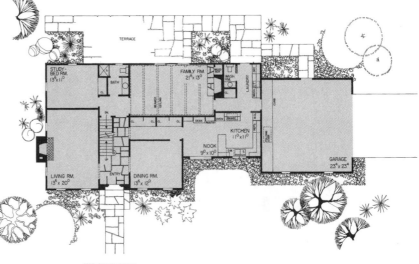

FIRST FLOOR

ORDER BLUEPRINTS 24 HOURS, 7 DAYS A WEEK, AT 1-800-521-6797

THE EASTERN SEABOARD
STYLISH CAPE COD HOMES

Cape Cods are among the most popular American designs of all time. This moderately sized 11/2-story plan is symmetrically beautiful. The traditional central foyer leads to a formal living area on the left and a study (or additional bedroom) on the right. A bay-windowed dining room is located between the spacious kitchen and the living room. A family room with a beam ceiling and raised-hearth fireplace offers access to the rear terrace through sliding glass doors. Dormer windows grace two of the three bedrooms on the second floor. The family bedrooms share a full bath. The master bedroom contains a private bath with a dressing area.

plan # HPK0200126

STYLE: CAPE COD
FIRST FLOOR: 1,157 SQ. FT.
SECOND FLOOR: 875 SQ. FT.
TOTAL: 2,032 SQ. FT.
BEDROOMS: 4
BATHROOMS: 2½
WIDTH: 60' - 0"
DEPTH: 34' - 0"
FOUNDATION: BASEMENT

SEARCH ONLINE @ EPLANS.COM

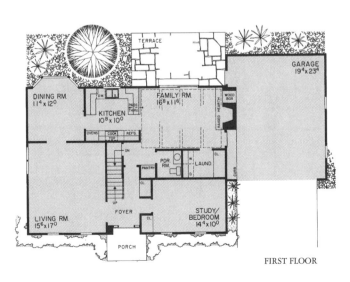

FIRST FLOOR

SECOND FLOOR

THE EASTERN SEABOARD
STYLISH CAPE COD HOMES

This updated country cottage will bring charm to any neighborhood. Dormers and shuttered windows are dressed up with pediments for added style on the facade. Straight ahead, the hearth-warmed family room awaits with a glorious wall of windows. This room flows into the breakfast nook on the left, which features French-door access to the rear and a serving bar to the kitchen. The kitchen enjoys ample pantry space and a unique angled sink. Hidden away at the right of the plan is a comfortable guest suite. Upstairs, find the magnificent master suite, complete with a curved ribbon of windows and its own private sitting room. At the right are two additional bedrooms and a full hall bath.

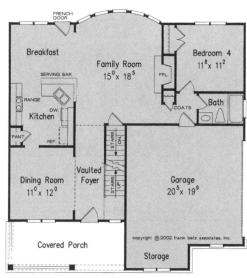

FIRST FLOOR

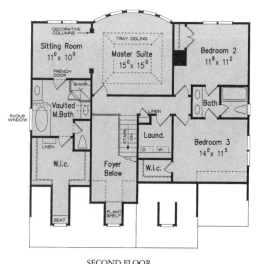

SECOND FLOOR

THE EASTERN SEABOARD
STYLISH CAPE COD HOMES

With overtones of Cape Cod styling, this lovely design presents dormer windows and shutters. The foyer opens to a spacious living room and dining room on the left and a den on the right. Because the den has an adjacent powder room, it might make a fine guest room. Fireplaces warm both the living room and the family room, which features a bay window and backyard access. Between the two living spaces sits a U-shaped kitchen with abundant counter space. An open-railed stair leads to a gallery on the second floor. On the right, two family bedrooms share a full bath. On the left is the master suite with a private bath and walk-in closet. Note the dormers in the two front bedrooms and the bay window in Bedroom 3.

plan # HPK0200128

STYLE: CAPE COD
FIRST FLOOR: 1,260 SQ. FT.
SECOND FLOOR: 1,064 SQ. FT.
TOTAL: 2,324 SQ. FT.
BEDROOMS: 3
BATHROOMS: 2½
WIDTH: 62' - 0"
DEPTH: 33' - 10"
FOUNDATION: BASEMENT

SEARCH ONLINE @ EPLANS.COM

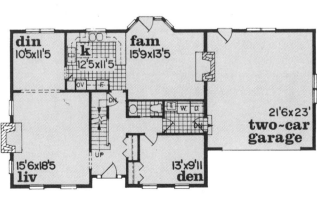

FIRST FLOOR

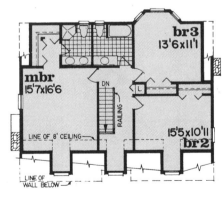

SECOND FLOOR

THE EASTERN SEABOARD
STYLISH CAPE COD HOMES

plan# HPK0200129

STYLE: COUNTRY COTTAGE
FIRST FLOOR: 1,211 SQ. FT.
SECOND FLOOR: 551 SQ. FT.
TOTAL: 1,762 SQ. FT.
BONUS SPACE: 378 SQ. FT.
BEDROOMS: 3
BATHROOMS: 2½
WIDTH: 64' - 4"
DEPTH: 39' - 4"
FOUNDATION: CRAWLSPACE,
BASEMENT

SEARCH ONLINE @ EPLANS.COM

An endearing and enduring American original that is straightforward and of spare design, yet warm, cozy, and uncomplicated, this home brings the past into sharp focus. The openness of the floor plan pairs the great room with the dining area for convenience and a modern flow. The island kitchen enjoys a view of the front property. The master suite features a large master bath with dual vanities, a compartmented toilet, and separate shower and tub. Two family bedrooms share a bath upstairs. Above the garage is future space that is easily converted into livable space as needed.

SECOND FLOOR

FIRST FLOOR

THE EASTERN SEABOARD
STYLISH CAPE COD HOMES

Beyond the simple traditional styling of this home's exterior are many of the amenities you want: a huge country kitchen with fireplace, an attached greenhouse/dining area, a media room off the two-story foyer, split-bedroom planning, and a second-floor lounge. The gathering room works well for both formal and casual occasions. It is expanded by a music alcove with built-in shelves. The master suite also includes an alcove area and has a well-appointed bath with dual walk-in closets, a whirlpool tub, vanity with two sinks, and a compartmented toilet. There are three bedrooms upstairs, sharing a full bath.

plan# HPK0200130

STYLE: CAPE COD
FIRST FLOOR: 1,953 SQ. FT.
SECOND FLOOR: 895 SQ. FT.
TOTAL: 2,848 SQ. FT.
BEDROOMS: 4
BATHROOMS: 2½
WIDTH: 63' - 0"
DEPTH: 56' - 8"
FOUNDATION: BASEMENT

SEARCH ONLINE @ EPLANS.COM

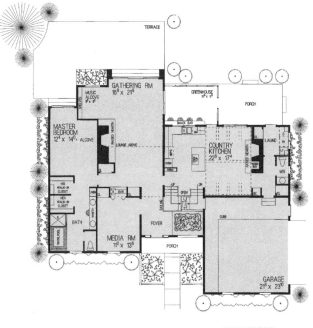

FIRST FLOOR

SECOND FLOOR

THE EASTERN SEABOARD
STYLISH CAPE COD HOMES

plan# HPK0200131

STYLE: COUNTRY COTTAGE
SQUARE FOOTAGE: 1,725
BONUS SPACE: 256 SQ. FT.
BEDROOMS: 3
BATHROOMS: 2
WIDTH: 58' - 0"
DEPTH: 54' - 6"
FOUNDATION: CRAWLSPACE,
BASEMENT

SEARCH ONLINE @ EPLANS.COM

This inviting Colonial-style home will capture your heart with a lovely facade and flowing floor plan. From the foyer and beyond, raised ceilings expand spaces visually. A vaulted great room is warmed by a cozy hearth and opens to the bayed breakfast nook. A serving-bar kitchen helps chefs prepare marvelous meals for any occasion and easily accesses the columned dining room. Tucked to the rear, the vaulted master suite enjoys light from radius windows and the comforts of a pampering spa bath. Two additional bedrooms are located to the far right, near a full bath and laundry room. Bonus space is available for an extra bedroom, study, or playroom—whatever your family desires.

THE EASTERN SEABOARD
STYLISH CAPE COD HOMES

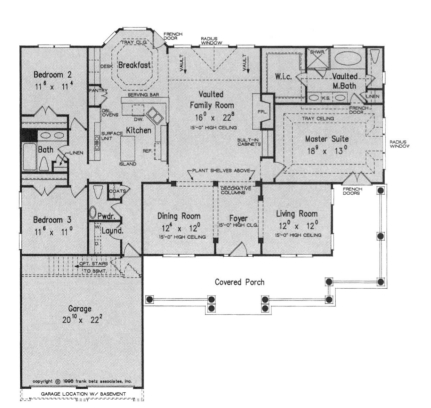

plan# HPK0200132

STYLE: COUNTRY COTTAGE
SQUARE FOOTAGE: 2,170
BEDROOMS: 3
BATHROOMS: 2½
WIDTH: 63' - 6"
DEPTH: 61' - 0"
FOUNDATION: CRAWLSPACE,
BASEMENT

SEARCH ONLINE @ EPLANS.COM

Twin dormers frame an impressive entrance to this fine three-bedroom home. The covered front porch leads to a foyer flanked by formal living and dining rooms. The spacious family room—complete with a warming fireplace and built-ins—opens to the breakfast bay. The well-positioned kitchen, with an island, easily serves the formal and informal areas. The master suite has a tray ceiling in the sleeping area and a vaulted ceiling in the bath. The other two bedrooms flank a full bath with a double-bowl vanity.

THE EASTERN SEABOARD
STYLISH CAPE COD HOMES

SECOND FLOOR

This economical design delivers great exterior appeal and fine livability. In addition to kitchen eating space, there is a separate dining room with access to the rear terrace. The living room features a central fireplace. A powder room serves the first-floor bedroom or study. Two bedrooms with walk-in closets and a full bath with a double-bowl vanity occupy the second floor. A garage shelters the rear terrace.

FIRST FLOOR

THE EASTERN SEABOARD
STYLISH CAPE COD HOMES

SECOND FLOOR

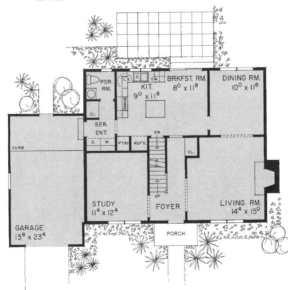

FIRST FLOOR

plan# HPK0200134

STYLE: CAPE COD
FIRST FLOOR: 964 SQ. FT.
SECOND FLOOR: 783 SQ. FT.
TOTAL: 1,747 SQ. FT.
BEDROOMS: 3
BATHROOMS: 2½
WIDTH: 48' - 0"
DEPTH: 32' - 0"
FOUNDATION: BASEMENT

SEARCH ONLINE @ EPLANS.COM

For those interested in both traditional charm and modern convenience, this Cape Cod home fits the bill. Enter the foyer and find a quiet study to the left and a living room with a fireplace to the right. Straight ahead lies the kitchen and breakfast room. The island countertop affords lots of room for meal preparation. The service entry introduces a laundry and powder room. Look for three bedrooms upstairs, including a pampering master suite with a whirlpool tub, separate shower, double-sink vanity, and walk-in closet.

THE EASTERN SEABOARD
STYLISH CAPE COD HOMES

plan # HPK0200135

STYLE: CAPE COD
FIRST FLOOR: 672 SQ. FT.
SECOND FLOOR: 571 SQ. FT.
TOTAL: 1,243 SQ. FT.
BEDROOMS: 3
BATHROOMS: 1½
WIDTH: 44' - 0"
DEPTH: 28' - 4"
FOUNDATION: BASEMENT

SEARCH ONLINE @ EPLANS.COM

The charming and affordable starter or retirement home presents an exterior finished in beveled siding and shutters. The combination living room/dining room sits on the right of the foyer and offers a fireplace and double-door access to the rear yard. A cozy yet adorable kitchen includes a window sink and direct access to a den or bedroom. On the second story, the master bedroom and Bedroom 2 each furnish built-in shelves and double-door closets. A full hall bath and linen closet are shared between the bedrooms. Note the single-car garage with storage space and second rear-yard entryway.`

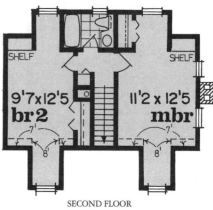

SHELF

9'7x12'5
br2

SHELF

11'2 x 12'5
mbr

SECOND FLOOR

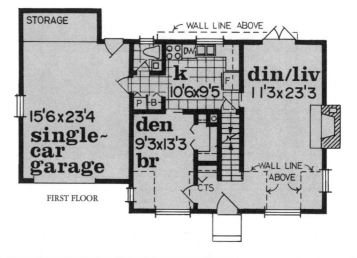

STORAGE

WALL LINE ABOVE

k
10'6x9'5

din/liv
11'3x23'3

15'6x23'4
single~
car
garage

den
9'3x13'3
br

WALL LINE ABOVE

CTS

FIRST FLOOR

plan# HPK0200136

STYLE: CAPE COD
FIRST FLOOR: 1,638 SQ. FT.
SECOND FLOOR: 1,006 SQ. FT.
TOTAL: 2,644 SQ. FT.
BEDROOMS: 5
BATHROOMS: 3½
WIDTH: 64' - 10"
DEPTH: 36' - 10"
FOUNDATION: BASEMENT

SEARCH ONLINE @ EPLANS.COM

SECOND FLOOR

This cozy home has over 2,600 square feet of livable floor area! And the manner in which this space is put to work to function conveniently for the large family is worth studying. Imagine five bedrooms, three full baths, living, dining, and family rooms. Note the large U-shaped kitchen and snack bar. Enjoy the morning in the nearby breakfast nook, which overlooks the terrace.

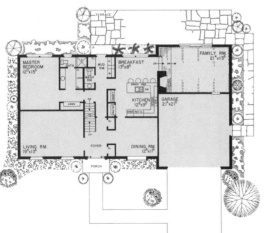

FIRST FLOOR

THE EASTERN SEABOARD
STYLISH CAPE COD HOMES

plan# HPK0200137

STYLE: EUROPEAN COTTAGE
FIRST FLOOR: 1,177 SQ. FT.
SECOND FLOOR: 457 SQ. FT.
TOTAL: 1,634 SQ. FT.
BONUS SPACE: 249 SQ. FT.
BEDROOMS: 3
BATHROOMS: 2½
WIDTH: 41' - 0"
DEPTH: 48' - 4"
FOUNDATION: CRAWLSPACE,
BASEMENT

SEARCH ONLINE @ EPLANS.COM

Influenced by Early American architecture, this petite rendition offers all of the amenities you love in a space designed for small lots. A two-story foyer is lit by surrounding sidelights and a multipane dormer window. The dining room flows conveniently into the efficient kitchen, which opens to the breakfast nook, brightened by sliding glass doors. The vaulted family room is warmed by an extended-hearth fireplace. Past a well-concealed laundry room, the master suite pampers with a vaulted spa bath and immense walk-in closet. Two bedrooms upstairs access future bonus space.

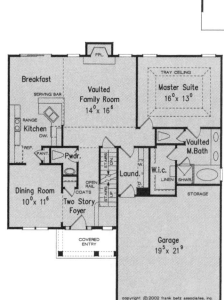

SECOND FLOOR

FIRST FLOOR

ORDER BLUEPRINTS 24 HOURS, 7 DAYS A WEEK, AT 1-800-521-6797

THE EASTERN SEABOARD
STYLISH CAPE COD HOMES

The garage wing of this Cape Cod closely resembles the main dwelling: narrow clapboards, shutters, and lintels over the multipane windows all match exactly. A narrow, shaded porch leads into the family room, which has twin bookcases framing the raised hearth as well as a rustic beam ceiling. The study downstairs easily converts to a guest bedroom and is conveniently served by a bath that boasts its own shower. This bath opens to the back hall so that it can be reached easily from the back rooms in the house. Two of the upstairs bedrooms have both dressing rooms and walk-in closets. The secondary bedrooms can, like the master bedroom, be opened up into one commodious room by removing the wall in between them.

plan# HPK0200138

STYLE: CAPE COD
FIRST FLOOR: 1,344 SQ. FT.
SECOND FLOOR: 948 SQ. FT.
TOTAL: 2,292 SQ. FT.
BEDROOMS: 3
BATHROOMS: 3
WIDTH: 74' - 0"
DEPTH: 35' - 4"
FOUNDATION: BASEMENT

SEARCH ONLINE @ EPLANS.COM

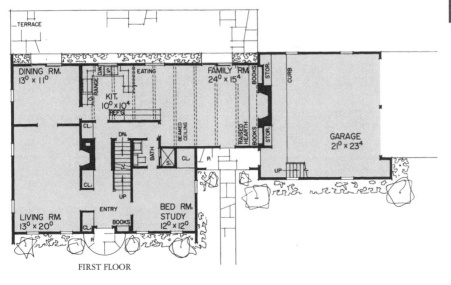

FIRST FLOOR

SECOND FLOOR

THE EASTERN SEABOARD
STYLISH CAPE COD HOMES

plan# HPK0200139

STYLE: CAPE COD
FIRST FLOOR: 873 SQ. FT.
SECOND FLOOR: 481 SQ. FT.
TOTAL: 1,354 SQ. FT.
BEDROOMS: 3
BATHROOMS: 2
WIDTH: 51' - 6"
DEPTH: 31' - 8"
FOUNDATION: BASEMENT

SEARCH ONLINE @ EPLANS.COM

A siding exterior with a covered porch, gabled roof, and a breezeway combine to create a fashionable home. Perfect for full-time family living or as a summer cottage, this 1½-story design offers an open living room and dining area, U-shaped kitchen, separate laundry room, and first-floor master suite. A large sliding glass door provides access from the dining area to the rear yard, offering a favorable indoor/outdoor relationship. Two bedrooms and a full bath are available on the second floor.

Bath

Bedroom
12'3" x 12'2"

Bedroom
12'6" x 12'2"

SECOND FLOOR

Patio

Breeze Way

Garage
12' x 21'

Dining
10'1" x 9'7"

Kitchen
8'7" x 8'8"

Laun.

Living Room
15'8" x 14'

Hall

Bath

WALK-IN CLOSET

STAIRS DN

STAIRS UP

Master Bedroom
12'6" x 14'6"

Porch

FIRST FLOOR

THE EASTERN SEABOARD
STYLISH CAPE COD HOMES

A covered porch and siding facade add color and dimension to this delightful 1½-story home. A convenient floor plan offers a favorable first impression. Turned stairs with rich wood finishes, a grand opening to the great room, fireplace wall as a focal point, and the introduction of natural light with the multiple windows combine to add spectacular design elements. A secondary hall offers convenient access to the kitchen and master suite. The large breakfast area and open kitchen, with island, create a delightful family work and gathering area. A first-floor master suite with tray ceiling, private bath, and walk-in closet creates a luxurious retreat. The second floor balcony offers a breathtaking view to the open foyer and leads to two additional bedrooms, bath, and storage space.

plan # HPK0200140

STYLE: COUNTRY COTTAGE
FIRST FLOOR: 1,263 SQ. FT.
SECOND FLOOR: 434 SQ. FT.
TOTAL: 1,697 SQ. FT.
BEDROOMS: 3
BATHROOMS: 2½
WIDTH: 55' - 2"
DEPTH: 57' - 3"
FOUNDATION: BASEMENT

SEARCH ONLINE @ EPLANS.COM

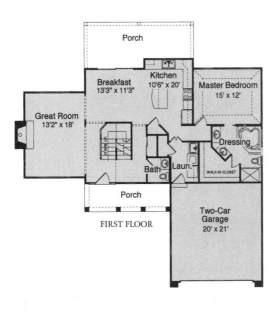

FIRST FLOOR

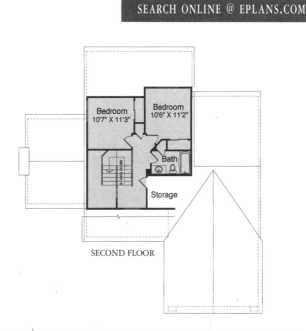

SECOND FLOOR

THE EASTERN SEABOARD
STYLISH CAPE COD HOMES

plan# HPK0200141

STYLE: CAPE COD
FIRST FLOOR: 2,188 SQ. FT.
SECOND FLOOR: 858 SQ. FT.
TOTAL: 3,046 SQ. FT.
BEDROOMS: 3
BATHROOMS: 3½ + ½
WIDTH: 106' - 8"
DEPTH: 32' - 0"
FOUNDATION: BASEMENT

SEARCH ONLINE @ EPLANS.COM

REAR EXTERIOR

Luxury is evident throughout this design, beginning with the elegantly proportioned dining room and living room. The country kitchen is spacious, with a U-shaped work area and an island cooktop at one end, an eating area and built-ins at the other, and a fireplace that provides the central focus. Far from the hustle and bustle is the secluded master bedroom. Curl up with a good book in the adjoining lounge or pamper yourself in the relaxing whirlpool tub. A handy laundry room, a washroom, and a mud area are near the three-car garage. Two second-floor bedrooms each enjoy private baths and share a lounge area.

SECOND FLOOR

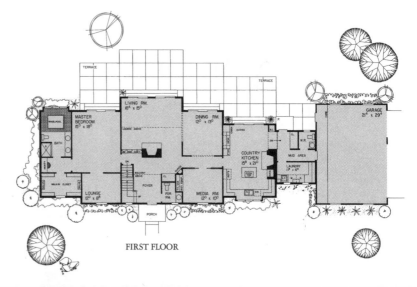

FIRST FLOOR

THE EASTERN SEABOARD
STYLISH CAPE COD HOMES

plan# HPK0200142

STYLE: CAPE COD
FIRST FLOOR: 2,563 SQ. FT.
SECOND FLOOR: 552 SQ. FT.
TOTAL: 3,115 SQ. FT.
BEDROOMS: 4
BATHROOMS: 2½ + ½
WIDTH: 87' - 8"
DEPTH: 68' - 8"
FOUNDATION: BASEMENT

SEARCH ONLINE @ EPLANS.COM

This fine example of a rambling Cape Cod house illustrates how delightful this style of home can be. This plan delivers exceptional country-estate livability. Both formal and informal living are covered with a large living room with a fireplace and even larger family room with another fireplace, a wet bar, and beamed ceiling. The kitchen and dining room are accented by a charming solarium, which also lights the master bedroom. A secondary bedroom or study opens off the foyer. Upstairs, two additional bedrooms share a full bath. The two-car garage connects to the main house via a convenient laundry room.

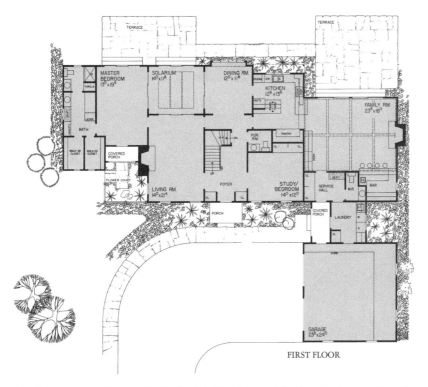

FIRST FLOOR

SECOND FLOOR

THE EASTERN SEABOARD
STYLISH CAPE COD HOMES

Here is a good example of how the historic half-house may have grown as its various appendages were attached. The result is a well-proportioned and practical facade. This 20th-Century version can be built all at one time. There is also the option of leaving the second floor unfinished for completion at a later date when family requirements change or finances improve. In this plan, the two most frequently used rooms are located to the rear of the house and function with the rear yard. The living room provides a formal conversation spot before the fireplace.

REAR EXTERIOR

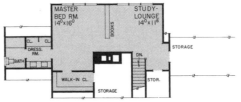

SECOND FLOOR

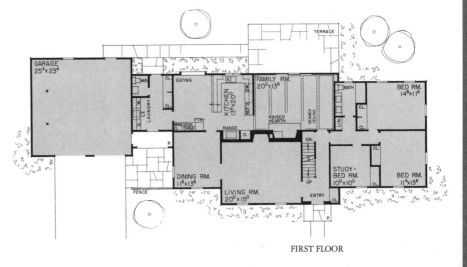

FIRST FLOOR

THE EASTERN SEABOARD
STYLISH CAPE COD HOMES

REAR EXTERIOR

plan# HPK0200144

STYLE: CAPE COD
FIRST FLOOR: 1,182 SQ. FT.
SECOND FLOOR: 708 SQ. FT.
TOTAL: 1,890 SQ. FT.
BEDROOMS: 3
BATHROOMS: 2
WIDTH: 80' - 0"
DEPTH: 35' - 0"
FOUNDATION: BASEMENT

SEARCH ONLINE @ EPLANS.COM

Historically referred to as a "half house," this authentic adaptation has its roots in the heritage of New England. With completion of the second floor, the growing family doubles its sleeping capacity. Notice that both the family and living rooms have a fireplace. Don't overlook the many built-in units featured throughout the plan.

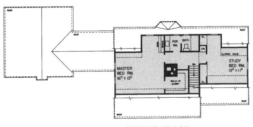

SECOND FLOOR

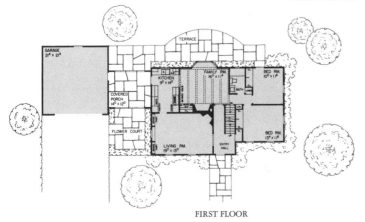

FIRST FLOOR

THE EASTERN SEABOARD
STYLISH CAPE COD HOMES

plan# HPK0200145

STYLE: CAPE COD
FIRST FLOOR: 1,141 SQ. FT.
SECOND FLOOR: 630 SQ. FT.
TOTAL: 1,771 SQ. FT.
BEDROOMS: 4
BATHROOMS: 2
WIDTH: 75' - 0"
DEPTH: 37' - 0"
FOUNDATION: BASEMENT

SEARCH ONLINE @ EPLANS.COM

This New England adaptation has a lot to offer. There is a U-shaped kitchen, family-dining room, four bedrooms, two full baths, fireplace, covered porch, and two-car garage. A delightful addition to any neighborhood.

SECOND FLOOR

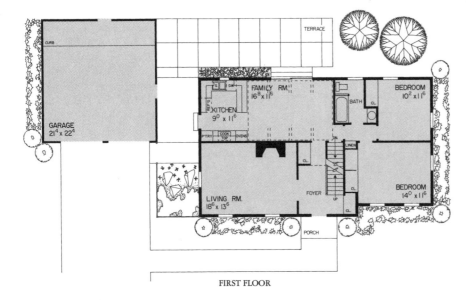

FIRST FLOOR

REAR EXTERIOR

SECOND FLOOR

plan# HPK0200146

STYLE: CAPE COD
FIRST FLOOR: 884 SQ. FT.
SECOND FLOOR: 598 SQ. FT.
TOTAL: 1,482 SQ. FT.
BEDROOMS: 4
BATHROOMS: 2
WIDTH: 58' - 0"
DEPTH: 24' - 5"
FOUNDATION: BASEMENT

SEARCH ONLINE @ EPLANS.COM

Build this home as a one-story starter, then finish the upper level as needs and budget dictate. The first level provides great livability in just under 900 square feet. The large living room has a bright multipane window and entry to the kitchen/dining area and the central hall. Access a rear terrace through sliding glass doors in the dining area. Two bedrooms have wall closets and share the use of a main bath with linen closet. If you choose to finish upper-level space, you'll gain two bedrooms and a full bath. Each bedroom has a wall closet and a dressing alcove, plus a built-in chest. A two-car garage has side access and a lovely window box at its multipane window.

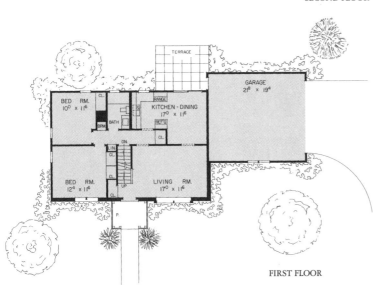

FIRST FLOOR

THE EASTERN SEABOARD
STYLISH CAPE COD HOMES

plan# HPK0200147

STYLE: CAPE COD
FIRST FLOOR: 919 SQ. FT.
SECOND FLOOR: 535 SQ. FT.
TOTAL: 1,454 SQ. FT.
BEDROOMS: 2
BATHROOMS: 2½
WIDTH: 34' - 4"
DEPTH: 30' - 0"
FOUNDATION: BASEMENT

SEARCH ONLINE @ EPLANS.COM

Compact enough for even the smallest lot, this cozy design provides comfortable living space for a small family. At the heart of the plan is a spacious country kitchen. It features a cooking island/snack bar and a dining area that opens to a house-wide rear terrace. The nearby dining room also opens to the terrace. At the front of the plan is the living room, warmed by a fireplace. Across the centered foyer is a cozy study. Two second-floor bedrooms are serviced by two baths. Note the first-floor powder room and storage closet located next to the side entrance.

SECOND FLOOR

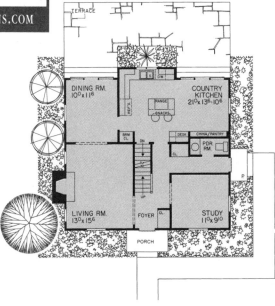

FIRST FLOOR

plan # HPK0200148

STYLE: CAPE COD
SQUARE FOOTAGE: 1,102
BEDROOMS: 2
BATHROOMS: 1
WIDTH: 51' - 4"
DEPTH: 31' - 0"
FOUNDATION: SLAB, CRAWLSPACE,
BASEMENT

SEARCH ONLINE @ EPLANS.COM

All the charms of a Cape Cod home are offered here in a sizeable footprint that is ideal for a narrow lot. The foyer opens to the spacious living room where a delightful fireplace adds warmth and atmosphere. The galley kitchen-dinette adjoins the formal dining room for efficiency in design. The two bedrooms find privacy in the rear sharing a full bath.

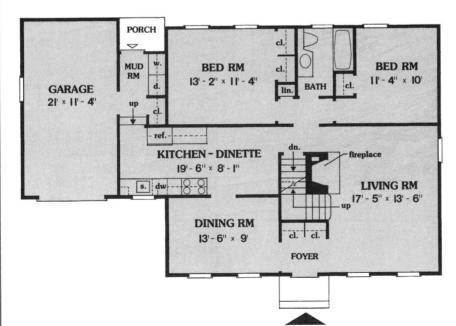

THE EASTERN SEABOARD

STYLISH CAPE COD HOMES

plan(#) HPK0200149

STYLE: CAPE COD
FIRST FLOOR: 960 SQ. FT.
SECOND FLOOR: 733 SQ. FT.
TOTAL: 1,693 SQ. FT.
BEDROOMS: 3
BATHROOMS: 2½
WIDTH: 32' - 0"
DEPTH: 30' - 0"
FOUNDATION: BASEMENT

SEARCH ONLINE @ EPLANS.COM

This efficient Saltbox design includes three bedrooms and two full baths upstairs, plus a handy powder room on the first floor. A large living room in the front of the home features a fireplace. The rear of the home is left open, with room for the kitchen with a snack bar, breakfast area with a fireplace, and dining room with outdoor access. If you wish, use the breakfast area as an all-purpose dining area and turn the dining room into a library or sitting room.

SECOND FLOOR

REAR EXTERIOR

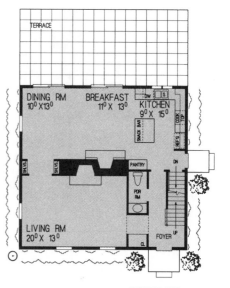

FIRST FLOOR

ORDER BLUEPRINTS 24 HOURS, 7 DAYS A WEEK, AT 1-800-521-6797

THE EASTERN SEABOARD
STYLISH CAPE COD HOMES

This charming Cape Cod maximizes style and use of space. The living room features a corner fireplace and a built-in curio cabinet. Nearby, the dining room is highlighted with a built-in china closet and access to the rear grounds. A warming fireplace shares space with the efficient kitchen and dining area. First-floor master suites are rarely found in Cape Cod-style homes, and this one is exceptional. The master suite combines with a master bath including a whirlpool tub, separate shower, and a walk-in closet. The second floor comprises two family bedrooms sharing a full bath.

plan # HPK0200150

STYLE: CAPE COD
FIRST FLOOR: 1,064 SQ. FT.
SECOND FLOOR: 582 SQ. FT.
TOTAL: 1,646 SQ. FT.
BEDROOMS: 3
BATHROOMS: 2
WIDTH: 38' - 0"
DEPTH: 28' - 0"
FOUNDATION: BASEMENT

SEARCH ONLINE @ EPLANS.COM

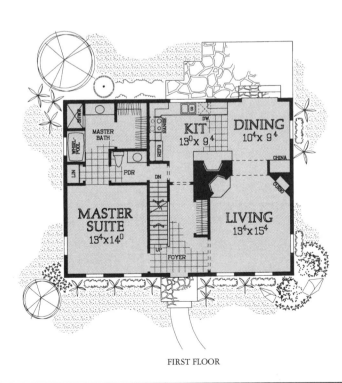

FIRST FLOOR

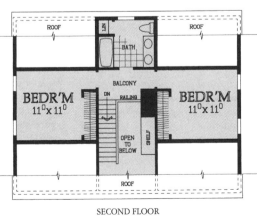

SECOND FLOOR

THE EASTERN SEABOARD
STYLISH CAPE COD HOMES

ALTERNATE FRONT EXTERIOR

plan# HPK0200151

STYLE: CAPE COD
FIRST FLOOR: 1,016 SQ. FT.
SECOND FLOOR: 766 SQ. FT.
TOTAL: 1,782 SQ. FT.
BEDROOMS: 3
BATHROOMS: 2½
WIDTH: 33' - 0"
DEPTH: 30' - 0"
FOUNDATION: BASEMENT

SEARCH ONLINE @ EPLANS.COM

Here's an expandable Colonial with a full measure of Cape Cod charm. Saltbox shapes and modular structures popular in early America enjoyed a revival at the turn of the century and have come to life again—this time with added square footage and some very comfortable amenities. Upstairs, a spacious master suite shares a gallery hall, which leads to two family bedrooms and sizable storage space. The expanded version of the basic plan adds a study wing to the left of the foyer as well as an attached garage with a service entrance to the kitchen.

REAR EXTERIOR

ALTERNATE REAR EXTERIOR

SECOND FLOOR

ALTERNATE SECOND FLOOR

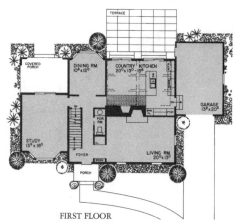

FIRST FLOOR

ALTERNATE FIRST FLOOR

THE LAP OF LUXURY
STYLISH, AMENITY-FILLED DREAM HOMES

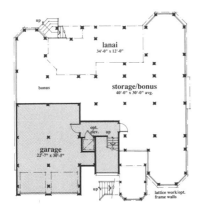

REAR EXTERIOR

SECOND FLOOR

BASEMENT

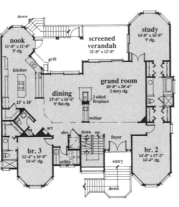

FIRST FLOOR

plan # HPK0200152

STYLE: FLORIDIAN
FIRST FLOOR: 2,725 SQ. FT.
SECOND FLOOR: 1,418 SQ. FT.
TOTAL: 4,143 SQ. FT.
BEDROOMS: 4
BATHROOMS: 5½
WIDTH: 61' - 4"
DEPTH: 62' - 0"
FOUNDATION: ISLAND BASEMENT

SEARCH ONLINE @ EPLANS.COM

Florida living takes off in this inventive design. A grand room gains attention as a superb entertaining area. A see-through fireplace here connects this room to the dining room. In the study, quiet time is assured—or slip out the doors and onto the veranda for a breather. A full bath connects the study and Bedroom 2. Bedroom 3 sits on the opposite side of the house and enjoys its own bath. The kitchen features a large work island and a connecting breakfast nook. Upstairs, the master bedroom suite contains His and Hers baths, a see-through fireplace, and access to an upper deck. A guest bedroom suite is located on the other side of the upper floor.

THE LAP OF LUXURY
STYLISH, AMENITY-FILLED DREAM HOMES

plan # HPK0200153

STYLE: TRADITIONAL
FIRST FLOOR: 2,285 SQ. FT.
SECOND FLOOR: 1,395 SQ. FT.
TOTAL: 3,680 SQ. FT.
BONUS SPACE: 300 SQ. FT.
BEDROOMS: 3
BATHROOMS: 3½
WIDTH: 73' - 8"
DEPTH: 76' - 2"
FOUNDATION: SLAB

SEARCH ONLINE @ EPLANS.COM

Now here is a one-of-a-kind house plan. Step down from the raised foyer into the grand gallery where columns define the living room. This central living area boasts an enormous bow window with a fantastic view to the covered patio. The formal dining room is to the right and the lavish master suite sits on the left. The family gourmet will find an expansive kitchen beyond a pair of French doors on the right. The secluded family room completes this first level. An enormous den is found on the first landing above, to the left of the foyer. Two bedroom suites and a loft occupy the second floor.

REAR EXTERIOR

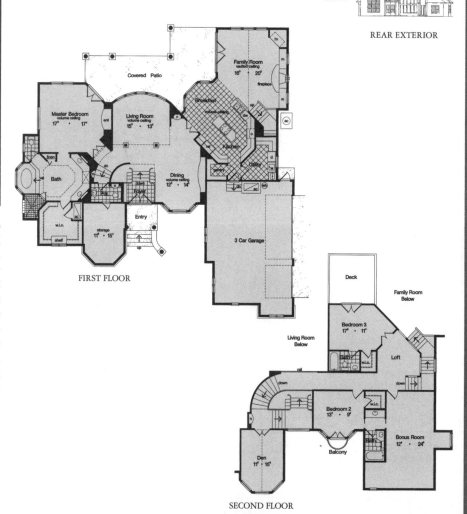

FIRST FLOOR

SECOND FLOOR

THE LAP OF LUXURY
STYLISH, AMENITY-FILLED DREAM HOMES

© HOME DESIGN SERVICES, INC.   J.N.HANSEN P.T.L.

A mixture of hipped and gabled rooflines lends this design an air of Old World sophistication. A raised foyer leads into a living room graced with a volume ceiling and a wall of windows that overlooks the covered patio. The large master bedroom boasts a volume ceiling, French doors to the covered patio, a private sitting area, a fireplace, two walk-in closets, and a spacious private bath. The vaulted family room enjoys a central fireplace, built-ins, and an abundance of windows. Enjoy the large island kitchen that leads to a window-filled breakfast area and and sports a convenient utility room. A grand staircase ascends to the sleeping quarters above, including three family bedrooms, a vaulted media room, and a loft and balcony that overlooks the family and living rooms below. Bedroom 4 is graced with a private deck and bath; Bedrooms 2 and 3 share a walk-through bath.

plan# HPK0200154

STYLE: TRANSITIONAL
FIRST FLOOR: 2,899 SQ. FT.
SECOND FLOOR: 1,472 SQ. FT.
TOTAL: 4,371 SQ. FT.
BEDROOMS: 4
BATHROOMS: 3½
WIDTH: 69' - 4"
DEPTH: 76' - 8"
FOUNDATION: SLAB

SEARCH ONLINE @ EPLANS.COM

FIRST FLOOR

SECOND FLOOR

THE LAP OF LUXURY
STYLISH, AMENITY-FILLED DREAM HOMES

plan# HPK0200155

STYLE: SEASIDE
FIRST FLOOR: 2,297 SQ. FT.
SECOND FLOOR: 1,929 SQ. FT.
TOTAL: 4,226 SQ. FT.
BEDROOMS: 4
BATHROOMS: 4½
WIDTH: 59' - 2"
DEPTH: 49' - 4"
FOUNDATION: ISLAND BASEMENT

SEARCH ONLINE @ EPLANS.COM

What a lovely Gulf Coast rendition! Living levels are elevated above double garages, and a portico and balcony decorate the front. Up the double staircase lies a covered double entry, which leads to a wide foyer with a dining room on the right and a guest room on the left. The grand room connects to the rear deck and the private study, which includes a fireplace. A U-shaped kitchen and a bayed breakfast room are on the right. The second floor includes three suites—all with private baths. The master suite is particularly spectacular, with double walk-in closets and a bath with a separate shower, tub, and dual sinks.

SECOND FLOOR

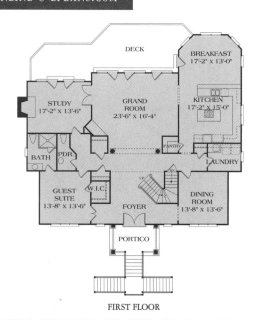

FIRST FLOOR

THE LAP OF LUXURY
STYLISH, AMENITY-FILLED DREAM HOMES

REAR EXTERIOR

UPPER LEVEL

MAIN LEVEL

LOWER LEVEL

plan# HPK0200156

STYLE: MEDITERRANEAN
MAIN LEVEL: 2,391 SQ. FT.
UPPER LEVEL: 922 SQ. FT.
LOWER LEVEL: 1,964 SQ. FT.
TOTAL: 5,277 SQ. FT.
BONUS SPACE: 400 SQ. FT.
BEDROOMS: 4
BATHROOMS: 4½
DEPTH: 85' - 6"
FOUNDATION: BASEMENT

SEARCH ONLINE @ EPLANS.COM

Here's an upscale multilevel plan with expansive rear views. The first floor provides an open living and dining area, defined by decorative columns and enhanced by natural light from tall windows. A breakfast area with a lovely triple window opens to a sunroom, which allows light to pour into the gourmet kitchen. The master wing features a tray ceiling in the bedroom, two walk-in closets, and an elegant private vestibule leading to a lavish bath. Upstairs, a reading loft overlooks the great room and leads to a sleeping area with two suites. A recreation room, exercise room, office, guest suite, and additional storage are available in the finished basement.

THE LAP OF LUXURY
STYLISH, AMENITY-FILLED DREAM HOMES

plan# HPK0200157

STYLE: NEO-ECLECTIC
FIRST FLOOR: 2,547 SQ. FT.
SECOND FLOOR: 1,637 SQ. FT.
TOTAL: 4,184 SQ. FT.
BONUS SPACE: 802 SQ. FT.
BEDROOMS: 4
BATHROOMS: 3½
WIDTH: 74' - 0"
DEPTH: 95' - 6"
FOUNDATION: CRAWLSPACE

SEARCH ONLINE @ EPLANS.COM

Double columns flank a raised loggia that leads to a beautiful two-story foyer. Flanking this elegance to the right is a formal dining room. Straight ahead, under a balcony and defined by yet more pillars, is the spacious grand room. A bow-windowed morning room and a gathering room feature a full view of the rear lanai and beyond. The master bedroom suite is lavish with its amenities, which include a bayed sitting area, direct access to the rear terrace, a walk-in closet, and a sumptuous bath.

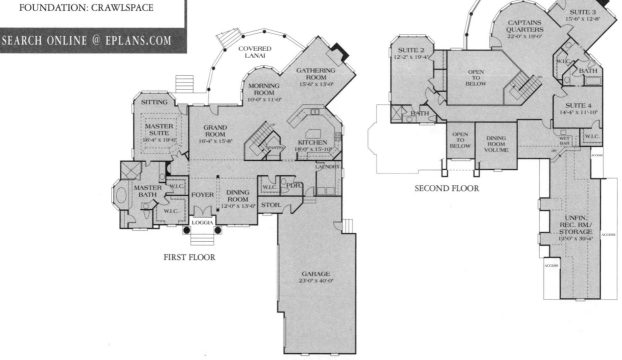

THE LAP OF LUXURY
STYLISH, AMENITY-FILLED DREAM HOMES

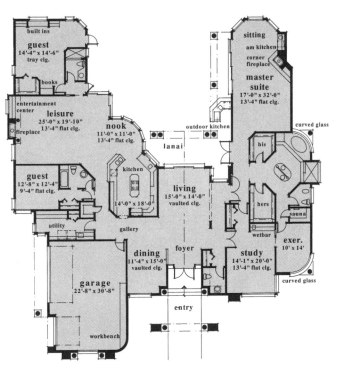

REAR EXTERIOR

plan # HPK0200158

STYLE: FLORIDIAN
SQUARE FOOTAGE: 4,565
BEDROOMS: 3
BATHROOMS: 3½
WIDTH: 88' - 0"
DEPTH: 95' - 0"
FOUNDATION: SLAB

SEARCH ONLINE @ EPLANS.COM

A freestanding entryway is the focal point of this luxurious residence. It has an arch motif that is carried through to the rear using a gabled roof and a vaulted ceiling from the foyer out to the lanai. The kitchen, which features a cooktop island and plenty of counter space, opens to the leisure area with a handy snack bar. Two guest suites with private baths are just off this casual living space. The master wing is truly pampering, stretching the entire length of the home. The suite has a large sitting area, a corner fireplace, and a morning kitchen. The bath features an island vanity, a raised tub with a curved glass wall overlooking a private garden, a sauna, and separate closets. An exercise room has a curved glass wall and a pocket door to the study, where a wet bar is ready to serve refreshments.

THE LAP OF LUXURY
STYLISH, AMENITY-FILLED DREAM HOMES

plan # HPK0200159

STYLE: NEO-ECLECTIC
FIRST FLOOR: 2,709 SQ. FT.
SECOND FLOOR: 2,321 SQ. FT.
TOTAL: 5,030 SQ. FT.
BEDROOMS: 4
BATHROOMS: 4½
WIDTH: 121' - 2"
DEPTH: 77' - 7"
FOUNDATION: CRAWLSPACE

SEARCH ONLINE @ EPLANS.COM

A huge foyer with a curved staircase welcomes you to this palatial four-bedroom home. On the main floor, you'll find the dining room, living room, den, family room, kitchen and dining nook, laundry room, one-and-a-half bathrooms, four-car garage, and lap pool. Terraces wrap partially around the home. On the second floor, the master suite includes a sitting room, deck, walk-in closet and compartmented bath. Three family bedrooms share two baths. The media room, also on the second floor, features a wet bar and overlooks the pool below.

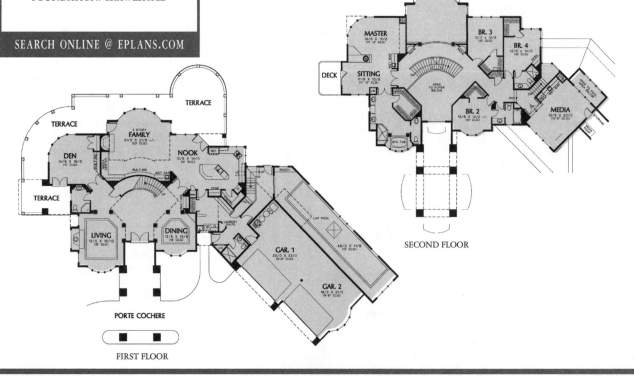

THE LAP OF LUXURY
STYLISH, AMENITY-FILLED DREAM HOMES

A level for everyone! On the first floor, there's a study with a full bath, a formal dining room, a grand room with a fireplace, and a fabulous kitchen with an adjacent morning room. The second floor contains three suites—each with a walk-in closet—two full baths, a loft, and a reading nook. A lavish master suite on the third floor is full of amenities, including His and Hers walk-in closets, a huge private bath, and a balcony. In the basement, casual entertaining takes off with a large gathering room, a home theater, and a spacious game room.

plan # HPK0200160

STYLE: CONTEMPORARY
FIRST FLOOR: 2,347 SQ. FT.
SECOND FLOOR: 1,800 SQ. FT.
THIRD FLOOR: 1,182 SQ. FT.
TOTAL: 5,329 SQ. FT.
BEDROOMS: 4
BATHROOMS: 4½
DEPTH: 76' - 4"
FOUNDATION: BASEMENT

SEARCH ONLINE @ EPLANS.COM

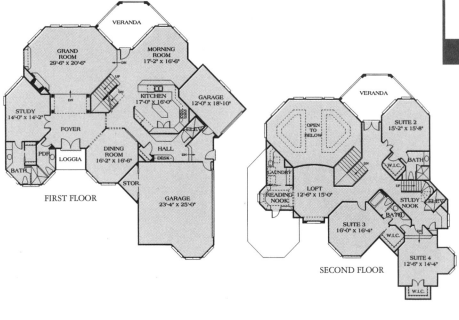

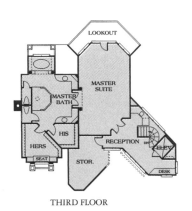

THE LAP OF LUXURY
STYLISH, AMENITY-FILLED DREAM HOMES

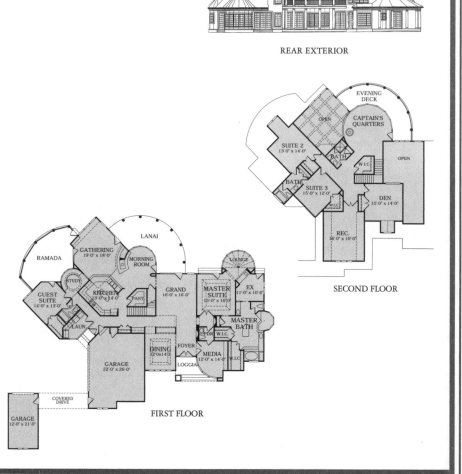

plan # HPK0200161

STYLE: MEDITERRANEAN
FIRST FLOOR: 3,322 SQ. FT.
SECOND FLOOR: 1,897 SQ. FT.
TOTAL: 5,219 SQ. FT.
BEDROOMS: 4
BATHROOMS: 4½
WIDTH: 106' - 6"
DEPTH: 89' - 10"
FOUNDATION: CRAWLSPACE

SEARCH ONLINE @ EPLANS.COM

A curved wall of windows leads to the entrance of this fine home. The lavish master suite features two walk-in closets, a deluxe bath with a separate tub and shower and two vanities, a separate lounge, and an exercise room. On the other end of the home, find the highly efficient kitchen, a spacious gathering room, a round morning room and study, and a quiet guest suite. The second level is equally deluxe with two suites, a recreation room, a quiet den, and a large open area called the captain's quarters that opens to an evening deck.

REAR EXTERIOR

SECOND FLOOR

FIRST FLOOR

THE LAP OF LUXURY
STYLISH, AMENITY-FILLED DREAM HOMES

Symmetry and stucco present true elegance on the facade of this five-bedroom home, and the elegance continues inside over four separate levels. Note the formal and informal gathering areas on the main level: the music room, the lake living room, the formal dining room, and the uniquely shaped breakfast room. The second level contains three large bedroom suites—one with its own bath—a spacious girl's room for play time, and an entrance room to the third-floor master suite. Lavish is the only way to describe this suite. Complete with His and Hers walk-in closets, a private balcony, an off-season closet, and a sumptuous bath, this suite is designed to pamper the homeowner.

plan# HPK0200162

STYLE: COUNTRY COTTAGE
FIRST FLOOR: 2,971 SQ. FT.
SECOND FLOOR: 2,199 SQ. FT.
THIRD FLOOR: 1,040 SQ. FT.
TOTAL: 6,210 SQ. FT.
BEDROOMS: 5
BATHROOMS: 4½
WIDTH: 84' - 4"
DEPTH: 64' - 11"
FOUNDATION: BASEMENT

SEARCH ONLINE @ EPLANS.COM

FIRST FLOOR

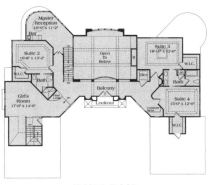

SECOND FLOOR

THIRD FLOOR

THE LAP OF LUXURY
STYLISH, AMENITY-FILLED DREAM HOMES

plan# HPK0200163

STYLE: MEDITERRANEAN
FIRST FLOOR: 2,035 SQ. FT.
SECOND FLOOR: 1,543 SQ. FT.
TOTAL: 3,578 SQ. FT.
BONUS SPACE: 366 SQ. FT.
BEDROOMS: 4
BATHROOMS: 4½
WIDTH: 62' - 0"
DEPTH: 76' - 0"
FOUNDATION: CRAWLSPACE

SEARCH ONLINE @ EPLANS.COM

Twin columns will usher you into the two-story foyer of this fine home. A quiet study to the left would make a great home office. Entertaining will be effortless, with a formal living room—complete with a fireplace—a formal dining room and a spacious family room, all opening onto a large covered porch—perfect for catching summer breezes. Don't miss the fireplace in the family room as well as the one on the porch. The kitchen will please the gourmet of the family, with its abundance of amenities. The lavish master suite is designed to pamper with a private deck, a huge walk-in closet, and a deluxe bath.

FIRST FLOOR

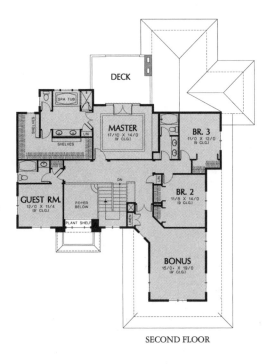

SECOND FLOOR

THE LAP OF LUXURY
STYLISH, AMENITY-FILLED DREAM HOMES

plan # HPK0200164

STYLE: PRAIRIE
MAIN LEVEL: 2,274 SQ. FT.
UPPER LEVEL: 1,380 SQ. FT.
LOWER LEVEL: 1,906 SQ. FT.
TOTAL: 5,560 SQ. FT.
BEDROOMS: 4
BATHROOMS: 3½
DEPTH: 63' - 0"
FOUNDATION: BASEMENT

SEARCH ONLINE @ EPLANS.COM

This multilevel contemporary home offers an array of winning combinations to make it truly unique and enjoyable. On the main level, the living and dining rooms are open to each other, creating ample space for entertaining and featuring a fireplace and a shared wet bar. The informal area combines a large family room, boasting another fireplace and outdoor access, with a sunny breakfast nook and an efficient kitchen. A secluded den and a powder room complete the main level. On the upper level, the master bedroom includes a separate sitting space, a spa bath, and an immense walk-in closet. It shares space with a guest suite that could also be used as an office or study. On the lower level, two family bedrooms share a full bath and enjoy a game room (with a third fireplace) and a wine cellar.

LOWER LEVEL

MAIN LEVEL

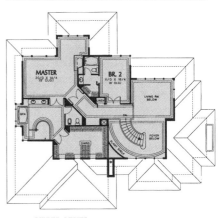

UPPER LEVEL

THE LAP OF LUXURY
STYLISH, AMENITY-FILLED DREAM HOMES

plan(#) HPK0200165

STYLE: FRENCH
FIRST FLOOR: 2,780 SQ. FT.
SECOND FLOOR: 878 SQ. FT.
TOTAL: 3,658 SQ. FT.
BEDROOMS: 4
BATHROOMS: 4
WIDTH: 68' - 3"
DEPTH: 89' - 1"
FOUNDATION: SLAB

SEARCH ONLINE @ EPLANS.COM

The symmetrical front of this home conceals an imaginatively asymmetrical floor plan beyond. A keeping room, a sitting area in the master bedroom, and a second bedroom all jut out from this home, forming interesting angles and providing extra window space. Two fireplaces, a game room, a study, and His and Hers bathrooms in the master suite are interesting elements in this home. The bayed kitchen, with a walk-in pantry and a center island with room for seating, is sure to lure guests and family alike. The open floor plan and two-story ceilings in the family room add a contemporary touch.

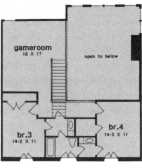

SECOND FLOOR

FIRST FLOOR

THE LAP OF LUXURY
STYLISH, AMENITY-FILLED DREAM HOMES

plan# HPK0200166

STYLE: FRENCH
FIRST FLOOR: 1,729 SQ. FT.
SECOND FLOOR: 2,312 SQ. FT.
TOTAL: 4,041 SQ. FT.
BEDROOMS: 4
BATHROOMS: 3½
WIDTH: 71' - 6"
DEPTH: 60' - 0"
FOUNDATION: CRAWLSPACE

SEARCH ONLINE @ EPLANS.COM

Entertaining will be a breeze for the owners of this imposing French manor home. Formal rooms open directly off the foyer, with a powder room nearby. Family members and friends may prefer the beam-ceilinged gathering room, with its fireplace and access to the covered front terrace. The kitchen, which easily serves both areas, features a walk-in pantry, an island cooktop, and a large breakfast nook. Upstairs, the master suite contains a sitting room and access to a private balcony, as well as a sumptuous bath. A reading area is centrally located for all four bedrooms, and a recreation room adds another opportunity for relaxation.

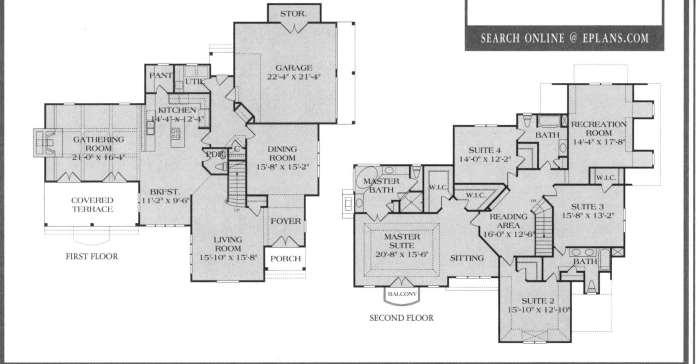

THE LAP OF LUXURY
STYLISH, AMENITY-FILLED DREAM HOMES

plan# HPK0200167

STYLE: FRENCH
FIRST FLOOR: 2,623 SQ. FT.
SECOND FLOOR: 935 SQ. FT.
TOTAL: 3,558 SQ. FT.
BEDROOMS: 4
BATHROOMS: 3
WIDTH: 67' - 6"
DEPTH: 79' - 3"
FOUNDATION: SLAB

SEARCH ONLINE @ EPLANS.COM

The street view of this fine four-bedroom home is just the start of its charm—the rear offers an expanse of windows perfect for riverside views and amenities abound inside. The foyer is flanked by a formal living room (or make it a study) and a formal dining room. The family room features a warming fireplace, built-in bookshelves, and a two-story wall of windows. The C-shaped kitchen is full of counter and cabinet space and includes a cooktop island and a large pantry. An adjacent breakfast room is surrounded by windows, offering early-morning sunshine. The first-floor master bedroom is quite lavish and includes two walk-in closets, two vanities, and a separate tub and shower. Finishing off this floor is a secluded bedroom and full bath, perfect for guests. Upstairs, two bedrooms share a bath and have access to a loft-like game room.

THE LAP OF LUXURY
STYLISH, AMENITY-FILLED DREAM HOMES

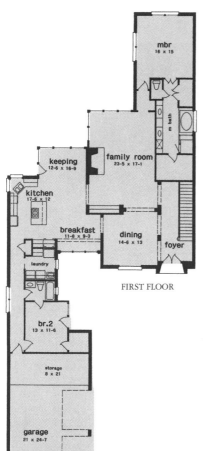

FIRST FLOOR

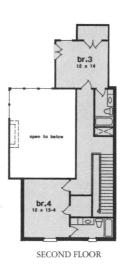

SECOND FLOOR

plan # HPK0200168

STYLE: FRENCH
FIRST FLOOR: 2,483 SQ. FT.
SECOND FLOOR: 889 SQ. FT.
TOTAL: 3,372 SQ. FT.
BEDROOMS: 4
BATHROOMS: 4
WIDTH: 49' - 10"
DEPTH: 120' - 11"
FOUNDATION: SLAB

SEARCH ONLINE @ EPLANS.COM

Designed for a narrow riverside lot, this two-story home is sure to please. The expanse of space occupied by the kitchen, keeping room, and breakfast room is amazing and will bring a feeling of spaciousness to any gathering. The nearby formal dining room will easily accommodate your dinner parties, with after-dinner conversation nicely flowing into the adjacent family room to gather in front of the fireplace. Sleeping quarters on the first floor include the deluxe master suite and a secluded bedroom and full bath past the kitchen. The second floor is complete with two good-sized bedrooms—each with walk-in closets and private baths.

THE LAP OF LUXURY
STYLISH, AMENITY-FILLED DREAM HOMES

REAR EXTERIOR

plan # HPK0200169

STYLE: FRENCH
SQUARE FOOTAGE: 3,032
BEDROOMS: 3
BATHROOMS: 3
WIDTH: 73' - 0"
DEPTH: 87' - 8"
FOUNDATION: SLAB

SEARCH ONLINE @ EPLANS.COM

This country estate is bedecked with all the details that pronounce its French origins. They include the study, family room, and keeping room. Dine in one of two areas—the formal dining room or the casual breakfast room. A large porch to the rear can be reached through the breakfast room or the master suite's sitting area. All three bedrooms in the plan have walk-in closets. Bedrooms 2 and 3 share a full bath that includes private vanities.

THE LAP OF LUXURY
STYLISH, AMENITY-FILLED DREAM HOMES

plan# HPK0200170

STYLE: FRENCH COUNTRY
SQUARE FOOTAGE: 3,430
BEDROOMS: 4
BATHROOMS: 3½
WIDTH: 78' - 9"
DEPTH: 79' - 4"
FOUNDATION: SLAB

SEARCH ONLINE @ EPLANS.COM

Wide-open windows grace this home and allow the rooms inside to enjoy natural light. Open living areas include a living room (or make it a study), a huge family room, a formal dining room, and a breakfast room. The island kitchen sits between the two dining areas for convenience. A wonderful solarium provides light and warmth to the family room and breakfast room. Two bedrooms are split from the master suite and share a full bath that includes private vanities. An additional bedroom on the right side of the plan has a private bath. Note the extra storage in the two-car garage.

sitting
7-2 x 9-5

master bath

mbr
17-1 x 18

solarium
20 x 9-6

brkfst
12-10 x 13-8

br.4
14-6 x 14-6

pantry

br.3
11-6 x 12-4

family
22 x 21

kit
13-6 x 15-4

laundry

butler

storage
3-6 x 16-2

br.2
12-6 x 11-6

living rm
(opt. study)
11-8 x 14

foyer

dining

garage
20-6 x 21

THE LAP OF LUXURY
STYLISH, AMENITY-FILLED DREAM HOMES

plan # HPK0200171

STYLE: FRENCH
SQUARE FOOTAGE: 3,230
BEDROOMS: 3
BATHROOMS: 3
WIDTH: 94' - 8"
DEPTH: 88' - 5"
FOUNDATION: SLAB

SEARCH ONLINE @ EPLANS.COM

A mini-estate with French Country details, this home preserves the beauty of historical design without sacrificing modern convenience. Through double doors, the floor plan opens from a central foyer flanked by a dining room and a study. The family room offers windows overlooking the rear yard and a fireplace. The master bedroom suite features a sitting room and bath fit for royalty. A smaller family bedroom has a full bath nearby. A third bedroom also enjoys a full bath.

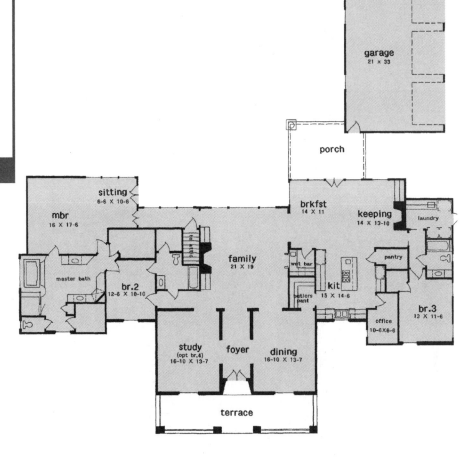

THE LAP OF LUXURY
STYLISH, AMENITY-FILLED DREAM HOMES

plan# HPK0200172

STYLE: FRENCH
FIRST FLOOR: 2,298 SQ. FT.
SECOND FLOOR: 731 SQ. FT.
TOTAL: 3,029 SQ. FT.
BEDROOMS: 4
BATHROOMS: 3
WIDTH: 71' - 10"
DEPTH: 78' - 0"
FOUNDATION: SLAB

SEARCH ONLINE @ EPLANS.COM

porch

brkfst
16 X 23-6

keeping

family
20-2 X 19

mbr
15 X 16-7

kit
12-9 X 15

dining
14 X 14

foyer

laundry

m bath

br.2
11-10 X 11

garage
18-1 X 21

11-1 X 21

terrace

FIRST FLOOR

br.3
12-2 X 14-11

br.4
11-6 X 11

SECOND FLOOR

Beautiful exterior detailing sets this home apart. A hipped roof, quaint dormers, French shutters, slightly arched windows and a stucco finish give this home European flair. Three sets of French doors open from the front terrace. The formal dining room is set to the left of the foyer. The family room, overlooked by a staircase to the second floor, accesses the rear through a set of double doors. The keeping room's fireplace warms both the breakfast room, which accesses a rear porch, and the nearby island kitchen. The master bedroom suite includes a private bath and walk-in closet. A second bedroom with a private bath is located on the opposite side of the home. Upstairs, two bedrooms share a full bath.

THE LAP OF LUXURY
STYLISH, AMENITY-FILLED DREAM HOMES

plan # HPK0200173

STYLE: CRAFTSMAN
FIRST FLOOR: 2,083 SQ. FT.
SECOND FLOOR: 1,013 SQ. FT.
TOTAL: 3,096 SQ. FT.
BEDROOMS: 4
BATHROOMS: 3½
WIDTH: 59' - 6"
DEPTH: 88' - 0"
FOUNDATION: SLAB

SEARCH ONLINE @ EPLANS.COM

This dream cabin captures the finest historic details in rooms furnished with comfort and style. A grand foyer features a radius staircase that decks out the entry hall and defines the wide-open interior. A formal dining room is served through a butler's pantry by a well-equipped kitchen. Casual space includes a leisure room that sports a corner fireplace, tray ceiling, and built-in media center. An outdoor kitchen makes it easy to enjoy life outside on the wraparound porch. The main-level master suite is suited with a spacious bedroom, two walk-in closets, and a lavish bath with separate vanities and a bumped-out whirlpool tub. Upstairs, two family bedrooms share a compartmented bath, and a guest suite boasts a roomy bath.

REAR EXTERIOR

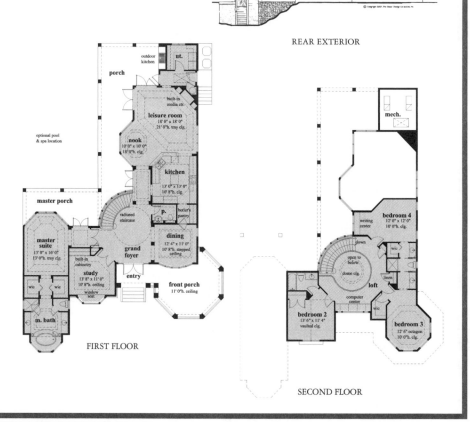

FIRST FLOOR

SECOND FLOOR

THE LAP OF LUXURY
STYLISH, AMENITY-FILLED DREAM HOMES

plan# HPK0200174

STYLE: CRAFTSMAN

FIRST FLOOR: 2,391 SQ. FT.

SECOND FLOOR: 1,539 SQ. FT.

TOTAL: 3,930 SQ. FT.

BEDROOMS: 3

BATHROOMS: 4½

WIDTH: 71' - 0"

DEPTH: 69' - 0"

FOUNDATION: ISLAND BASEMENT

SEARCH ONLINE @ EPLANS.COM

REAR EXTERIOR

SECOND FLOOR

BASEMENT

FIRST FLOOR

Climate is a key component of any mountain retreat, and outdoor living is an integral part of its design. This superior cabin features open and covered porches. A mix of match-stick details and rugged stone set off this lodge-house facade, concealing a well-defined interior. Windows line the breakfast bay and brighten the kitchen, which features a center cooktop island. A door leads out to a covered porch with a summer kitchen. The upper level features a secluded master suite with a spacious bath beginning with a double walk-in closet and ending with a garden view of the porch. A two-sided fireplace extends warmth to the whirlpool spa-style tub.

THE LAP OF LUXURY
STYLISH, AMENITY-FILLED DREAM HOMES

plan # HPK0200175

STYLE: CRAFTSMAN
MAIN LEVEL: 2,213 SQ. FT.
LOWER LEVEL: 1,333 SQ. FT.
TOTAL: 3,546 SQ. FT.
BONUS SPACE: 430 SQ. FT.
BEDROOMS: 4
BATHROOMS: 3½
DEPTH: 93' - 1"
FOUNDATION: BASEMENT

SEARCH ONLINE @ EPLANS.COM

Interesting window treatments highlight this stone-and-shake facade, but don't overlook the columned porch to the left of the portico. Arches outline the formal dining room and the family room, both of which are convenient to the island kitchen. Household chores are made easier by the placement of a pantry, powder room, laundry room, and office between the kitchen and the entrances to the side porch and garage. If your goal is relaxation, the breakfast room, screened porch, and covered deck are also nearby. The master suite features a beautiful bay, and three secondary bedrooms and a recreation room are on the lower level.

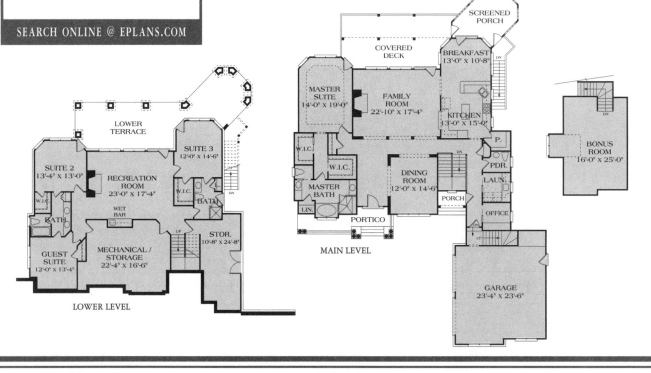

THE LAP OF LUXURY
STYLISH, AMENITY-FILLED DREAM HOMES

REAR EXTERIOR

THIRD FLOOR

DECK

SITTING
12'-4" x 8'-8"

BONUS
ROOM
12'-4" x 17'-4"

W.I.C.

BATH

plan # HPK0200176

STYLE: COUNTRY COTTAGE
FIRST FLOOR: 2,030 SQ. FT.
SECOND FLOOR: 1,967 SQ. FT.
THIRD FLOOR: 688 SQ. FT.
TOTAL: 4,685 SQ. FT.
BEDROOMS: 4
BATHROOMS: 5
WIDTH: 80' - 8"
DEPTH: 111' - 8"
FOUNDATION: CRAWLSPACE

SEARCH ONLINE @ EPLANS.COM

This Northwest Coastal/country-style home extends livability outside with its front and back porches and elevated deck. The first floor flows from the open family room and breakfast nook to the kitchen with U-shaped counters. The dining room opens to the kitchen and the foyer. In the front, a guest suite contains a private bath. Upstairs, the spacious master bedroom has a walk-in closet and access to the deck. The family bedrooms share a bath with the study. Attached to the main house by a breezeway, the garage includes an unfinished area above that can be converted to an apartment.

PORCH

BKFST.
10'-0" x 20'-4"

KITCHEN
15'-0" x 20'-4"

FAMILY
ROOM
20'-4" x 20'-0"

LAUNDRY

BATH

DINING
ROOM
16'-8" x 15'-0"

FOYER

GUEST
SUITE
17'-0" x 13'-0"

BATH

PORCH

BREEZEWAY

FIRST FLOOR

3-CAR
GARAGE
25'-4" x 34'-6"

DECK

DECK

COVERED
DECK

SUITE 2
14'-2" x 13'-6"

MASTER
SUITE
20'-6" x 17'-0"

W.I.C.

MASTER
BATH

DRESS.

BATH

STUDY
17'-0" x 20'-0"

SUITE 3
14'-6" x 13'-0"

DECK

SECOND FLOOR

UNFIN.
AREA
14'-0" x 34'-6"

THE LAP OF LUXURY
STYLISH, AMENITY-FILLED DREAM HOMES

plan # HPK0200177

STYLE: CRAFTSMAN
MAIN LEVEL: 2,932 SQ. FT.
LOWER LEVEL: 1,556 SQ. FT.
TOTAL: 4,488 SQ. FT.
BEDROOMS: 3
BATHROOMS: 3½ + ½
DEPTH: 82' - 11"
FOUNDATION: BASEMENT

SEARCH ONLINE @ EPLANS.COM

The interior of this home boasts high ceilings, a wealth of windows, and interestingly shaped rooms. A covered portico leads into a roomy foyer, which is flanked by an office/study, accessible through French doors. Just beyond the foyer, a huge, vaulted family room highlights columns decorating the entrance and positioned throughout the room. The island kitchen nestles close to the beautiful dining room, which features rear property views through the bay window and a nearby door to the terrace. The main level master suite enjoys two walk-in closets and a lavish bath, as well as access to a covered terrace. The lower level is home to the remaining bedrooms, including Suites 2 and 3, an abundance of storage, a recreation room, and a large mechanical/storage room.

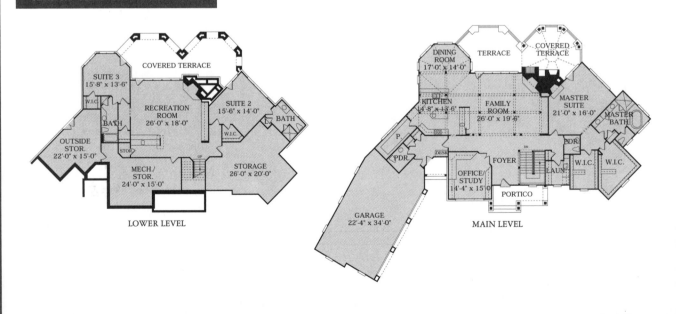

plan# HPK0200178

STYLE: CAPE COD
FIRST FLOOR: 2,914 SQ. FT.
SECOND FLOOR: 1,405 SQ. FT.
TOTAL: 4,319 SQ. FT.
BEDROOMS: 4
BATHROOMS: 3½
WIDTH: 139' - 0"
DEPTH: 78' - 2"
FOUNDATION: CRAWLSPACE

SEARCH ONLINE @ EPLANS.COM

What appears to be a rustic country cottage is in fact, upon closer inspection, a stunning Early American estate with the beauty and dignity that suggests it is already an established home. Upon entry through French doors, a grand foyer opens on the right to a stately dining room. The adjacent wet bar is also convenient to the airy island-cooktop kitchen. The living room and den flank the kitchen, both with fireplaces. The master suite is on the left with a vaulted ceiling and a resplendent bath. Upstairs, three generous bedrooms share two full baths. Unfinished space abounds—two storage areas and a studio apartment—ready for completion as your needs change

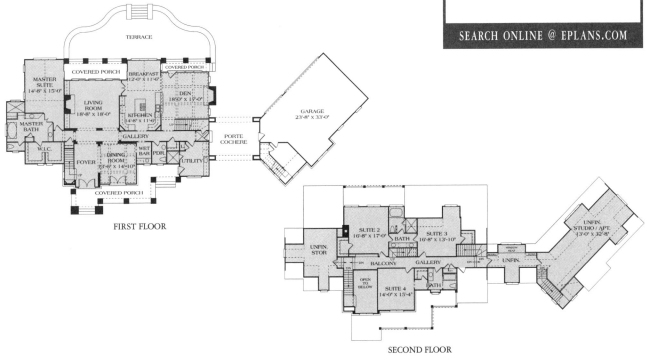

FIRST FLOOR

SECOND FLOOR

THE LAP OF LUXURY
STYLISH, AMENITY-FILLED DREAM HOMES

© 1998 Donald A. Gardner Architects, Inc.

SEARCH ONLINE @ EPLANS.COM

plan# HPK0200179

STYLE: EUROPEAN COTTAGE
MAIN LEVEL: 2,297 SQ. FT.
LOWER LEVEL: 1,212 SQ. FT.
TOTAL: 3,509 SQ. FT.
BEDROOMS: 5
BATHROOMS: 5½
DEPTH: 69' - 0"

REAR EXTERIOR

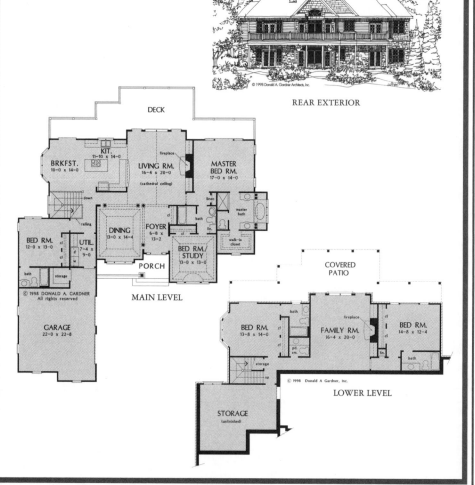

MAIN LEVEL

LOWER LEVEL

A variety of exterior materials and interesting windows combine with an unusual floor plan to make this an exceptional home. It is designed for a sloping lot, with full living quarters on the main level, but with two extra bedrooms and a family room added to the lower level. A covered porch showcases a wonderful dining-room window and an attractive front door. The living room, enhanced by a fireplace, adjoins the dining room for easy entertaining. The island kitchen and a bayed breakfast room are to the left. Three bedrooms on this level include one that could serve as a study and one as a master suite with dual vanities, a garden tub, and a walk-in closet. A deck on this floor covers the patio off the lower-level family room, which has its own fireplace.

THE LAP OF LUXURY
STYLISH, AMENITY-FILLED DREAM HOMES

REAR EXTERIOR

SECOND FLOOR

plan# HPK0200180

STYLE: BUNGALOW
FIRST FLOOR: 2,096 SQ. FT.
SECOND FLOOR: 892 SQ. FT.
TOTAL: 2,988 SQ. FT.
BEDROOMS: 3
BATHROOMS: 3½
WIDTH: 56' - 0"
DEPTH: 54' - 0"
FOUNDATION: BASEMENT

SEARCH ONLINE @ EPLANS.COM

Siding and shingles give this home a Craftsman look. The foyer opens to a short flight of stairs that leads to the great room, which features a lovely coffered ceiling, a fireplace, built-ins, and French doors to the rear veranda. To the left, the open, island kitchen enjoys a pass-through to the great room and easy service to the dining bay. The secluded master suite has two walk-in closets, a luxurious bath, and veranda access. Upstairs, two family bedrooms enjoy their own full baths and share a loft area.

BASEMENT

FIRST FLOOR

THE LAP OF LUXURY
STYLISH, AMENITY-FILLED DREAM HOMES

plan # HPK0200181

STYLE: SEASIDE
FIRST FLOOR: 1,512 SQ. FT.
SECOND FLOOR: 1,746 SQ. FT.
TOTAL: 3,258 SQ. FT.
BEDROOMS: 5
BATHROOMS: 4½
WIDTH: 63' - 6"
DEPTH: 62' - 6"
FOUNDATION: WALKOUT BASEMENT

SEARCH ONLINE @ EPLANS.COM

This engaging design blends the clean, sharp edges of the sophisticated shingle style with relaxed cottage details such as dovecote gables and flower boxes. The great room, with built-in bookshelves and a fireplace, opens to the kitchen and breakfast room, where a door leads to the deck. A spacious guest bedroom also accesses the deck and has an adjoining bath and a walk-in closet. Upstairs, a study area provides a built-in desk. A dramatic master suite includes a bath with double vanities, a garden tub, and a separate shower. Two bedrooms, one with a walk-in closet, share a full bath; a third features a private bath.

FIRST FLOOR

SECOND FLOOR

ORDER BLUEPRINTS 24 HOURS, 7 DAYS A WEEK, AT 1-800-521-6797

THE LAP OF LUXURY

STYLISH, AMENITY-FILLED DREAM HOMES

plan# HPK0200182

STYLE: SEASIDE
FIRST FLOOR: 1,635 SQ. FT.
SECOND FLOOR: 1,974 SQ. FT.
TOTAL: 3,609 SQ. FT.
BEDROOMS: 4
BATHROOMS: 3½
WIDTH: 70' - 6"
DEPTH: 77' - 4"
FOUNDATION: BASEMENT

SEARCH ONLINE @ EPLANS.COM

This stone-and-shingle facade complements this gambrel roof. Inside, a well-arranged interior features a center passageway with a straight stair running from front to back. On the first floor, the formal living/dining room leads to a side entry. On the right, the expansive great room features a massive hearth and access to a covered rear deck. The family will share casual meals in the breakfast room adjoining the kitchen. The upper floor includes four bedrooms, one an extravagant master suite with two walk-in closets. Bedrooms 2 and 3 share a full bath; Bedroom 4 has a private bath and two wall closets.

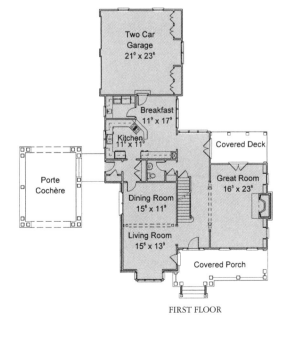

FIRST FLOOR

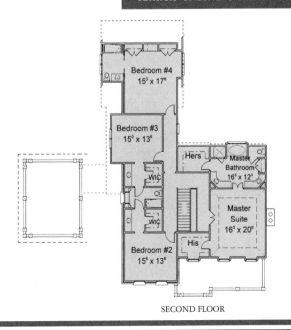

SECOND FLOOR

THE LAP OF LUXURY
STYLISH, AMENITY-FILLED DREAM HOMES

plan# HPK0200183

STYLE: COUNTRY COTTAGE
FIRST FLOOR: 1,886 SQ. FT.
SECOND FLOOR: 2,076 SQ. FT.
TOTAL: 3,962 SQ. FT.
BEDROOMS: 5
BATHROOMS: 4½
WIDTH: 49' - 0"
DEPTH: 75' - 0"
FOUNDATION: BASEMENT

SEARCH ONLINE @ EPLANS.COM

Perhaps the most dramatic feature of this lovely Colonial home is its magnificent master suite. Dominating the second level, it first offers a generously sized bedroom with a fireplace and doors leading to the deck. Next comes a private sitting room, opening to His and Hers walk-in closets; an opulent private bath follows. Three family bedrooms, one with a private bath, occupy the rest of the second level. The first level has many attractive features as well: a comfortable great room with deck access and a warming fireplace; a kitchen that conveniently serves a dining room and a breakfast room; a welcoming guest bedroom; and a study/office area.

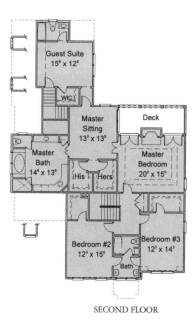

SECOND FLOOR

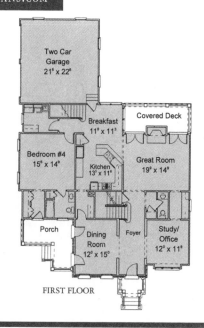

FIRST FLOOR

plan # HPK0200184

STYLE: COLONIAL
FIRST FLOOR: 1,567 SQ. FT.
SECOND FLOOR: 1,895 SQ. FT.
TOTAL: 3,462 SQ. FT.
BEDROOMS: 4
BATHROOMS: 3½
WIDTH: 63' - 0"
DEPTH: 53' - 6"
FOUNDATION: WALKOUT BASEMENT

SEARCH ONLINE @ EPLANS.COM

Although the facade may look like a quaint country cottage, this home's fine proportions contain formal living areas, including a dining room and a living room. At the back of the first floor you'll find a spacious kitchen and breakfast nook. A great room with a fireplace and bumped-out window makes everyday living very comfortable. A rear porch allows for outdoor dining and relaxation. Upstairs, four bedrooms include a master suite with lots of notable features. A boxed ceiling, lavish bath, large walk-in closet, and secluded sitting room (which would also make a nice study or exercise room) assure great livability.

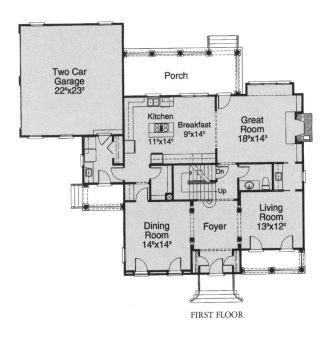

FIRST FLOOR

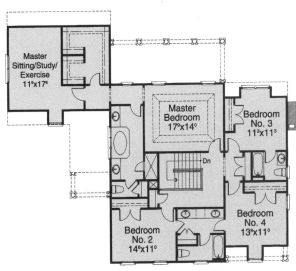

SECOND FLOOR

THE LAP OF LUXURY
STYLISH, AMENITY-FILLED DREAM HOMES

plan # HPK0200185

STYLE: COLONIAL
FIRST FLOOR: 2,348 SQ. FT.
SECOND FLOOR: 1,872 SQ. FT.
TOTAL: 4,220 SQ. FT.
BEDROOMS: 4
BATHROOMS: 3½ + ½
WIDTH: 90' - 4"
DEPTH: 44' - 8"
FOUNDATION: BASEMENT

SEARCH ONLINE @ EPLANS.COM

This classic Georgian design contains a variety of features that make it outstanding: a pediment gable with cornice work and dentils, beautifully proportioned columns, and a distinct window treatment. Inside the foyer, a stunning curved staircase introduces you to this Southern-style home. The first floor contains some special appointments: a fireplace in the living room and another fireplace and a wet bar in the gathering room. A study is offered towards the rear of the plan for convenient home office use. A gourmet island kitchen is open to a breakfast room with a pantry. Upstairs, an extension over the garage allows for a huge walk-in closet in the master suite and a full bath in one of the family bedrooms.

REAR EXTERIOR

SECOND FLOOR

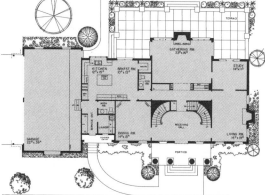

FIRST FLOOR

THE LAP OF LUXURY
STYLISH, AMENITY-FILLED DREAM HOMES

Double columns flank the grand portico of this fine two-story home. Inside, the foyer presents a formal living room. This room welcomes all with a beam ceiling and a wall of windows to the rear veranda. The C-shaped kitchen offers a work-surface island, a walk-in pantry, and easy access to the spacious gathering room. Located on the first floor for privacy, the master suite is lavish with its luxuries. Upstairs, two family suites—each with a walk-in closet—share a full bath, and the large guest suite features another walk-in closet as well as a private bath.

plan# HPK0200186

STYLE: TRADITIONAL
FIRST FLOOR: 2,538 SQ. FT.
SECOND FLOOR: 1,581 SQ. FT.
TOTAL: 4,119 SQ. FT.
BEDROOMS: 4
BATHROOMS: 3½
WIDTH: 67' - 7"
DEPTH: 84' - 5"
FOUNDATION: BASEMENT

SEARCH ONLINE @ EPLANS.COM

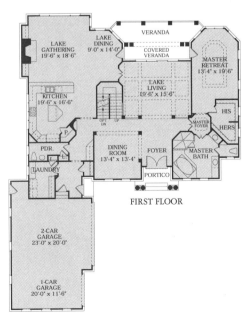

FIRST FLOOR

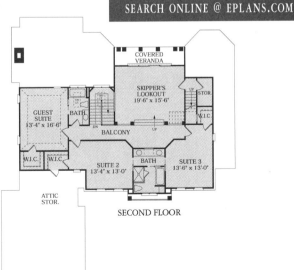

SECOND FLOOR

THE LAP OF LUXURY
STYLISH, AMENITY-FILLED DREAM HOMES

plan # HPK0200187

STYLE: PLANTATION
FIRST FLOOR: 2,033 SQ. FT.
SECOND FLOOR: 1,116 SQ. FT.
TOTAL: 3,149 SQ. FT.
BEDROOMS: 4
BATHROOMS: 3½
WIDTH: 71' - 0"
DEPTH: 56' - 0"
FOUNDATION: CRAWLSPACE, SLAB

SEARCH ONLINE @ EPLANS.COM

This large Southern-style home offers luxury to spare, inside and out. Decorative columns and tall arched windows along a raised porch welcome guests and introduce a grand two-story foyer. In the great room, picture the central fireplace glowing between graceful French doors which open to a rear porch and deck. Luxury abounds in the opulent master suite, complete with a sitting room that leads to a private rear porch and deck, a separate front porch and a master bath with a corner whirlpool tub. The gourmet kitchen and adjoining breakfast area share a private porch as well. Upstairs, a hall balcony connects three family bedrooms and two full baths.

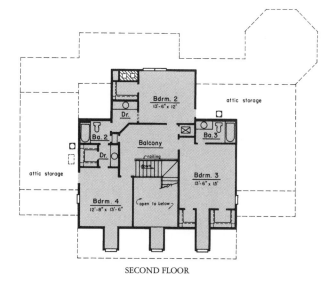

SECOND FLOOR

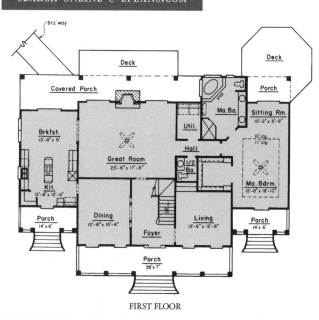

FIRST FLOOR

THE LAP OF LUXURY
STYLISH, AMENITY-FILLED DREAM HOMES

REAR EXTERIOR

plan # HPK0200188

STYLE: TRADITIONAL
FIRST FLOOR: 2,687 SQ. FT.
SECOND FLOOR: 1,630 SQ. FT.
TOTAL: 4,317 SQ. FT.
BONUS SPACE: 216 SQ. FT.
BEDROOMS: 4
BATHROOMS: 3
WIDTH: 87' - 1"
DEPTH: 76' - 7"
FOUNDATION: CRAWLSPACE

SEARCH ONLINE @ EPLANS.COM

Dormer windows complement classic square columns on this country estate home, gently flavored with a Southern-style facade. A two-story foyer opens to traditional rooms. Two columns announce the living room, which has a warming hearth. The formal dining room opens to the back covered porch, decked out with decorative columns. The first-floor master suite has His and Hers walk-in closets, an oversized shower, a whirlpool tub, and a windowed water closet, plus its own door to the covered porch. A well-appointed kitchen features a corner walk-in pantry and opens to a double-bay family room and breakfast area. Upstairs, each of two family bedrooms has a private vanity. A gallery hall leads past a study/computer room—with two window seats—to a sizable recreation area that offers a tower-room bay.

SECOND FLOOR

FIRST FLOOR

THE LAP OF LUXURY
STYLISH, AMENITY-FILLED DREAM HOMES

plan # HPK0200189

STYLE: STICK VICTORIAN
FIRST FLOOR: 4,383 SQ. FT.
SECOND FLOOR: 1,557 SQ. FT.
TOTAL: 5,940 SQ. FT.
BEDROOMS: 5
BATHROOMS: 5½
WIDTH: 148' - 8"
DEPTH: 120' - 5"
FOUNDATION: BASEMENT

SEARCH ONLINE @ EPLANS.COM

Victorian-inspired, this estate home is rife with details and grand appointments. The central foyer opens from double doors on the wrapping veranda and leads to a parlor on the right and a study on the left. The parlor shares a through-fireplace with the formal dining room. A keeping room at the back is open to the island kitchen. A service hall leads to the three-car garage, which has a full apartment above. A media room and the master suite round out the first level. The second level holds three bedrooms with three private baths. A terrace opens from double doors on the west gallery.

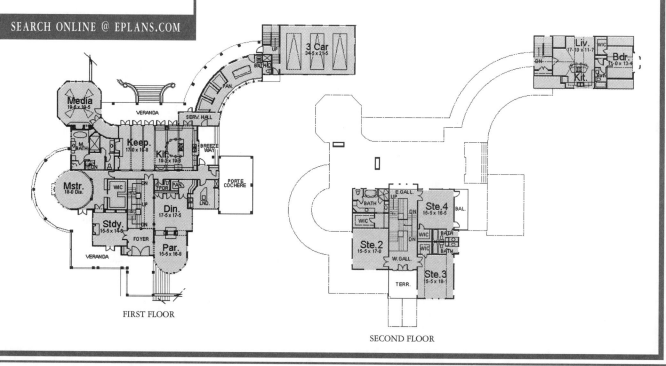

FIRST FLOOR

SECOND FLOOR

ORDER BLUEPRINTS 24 HOURS, 7 DAYS A WEEK, AT 1-800-521-6797

eplans.com

THE GATEWAY TO YOUR NEW HOME

Looking for more plans? Got questions?
Try our one-stop home plans resource—eplans.com.

We'll help you streamline the plan selection process, so your dreams can become reality faster than you ever imagined. From choosing your home plan and ideal location to finding an experienced contractor, eplans.com will guide you every step of the way.

Mix and match! Explore! At eplans.com you can combine all your top criteria to find your perfect match. Search for your ideal home plan by any or all of the following:

> Number of bedrooms or baths,
> Total square feet,
> House style,
> Cost.

With over 10,000 plans, the options are endless. Colonial, ranch, country, and Victorian are just a few of the house styles offered. Keep in mind your essential lifestyle features—whether to include a porch, fireplace, bonus room or main floor laundry room. And the garage—how many cars must it accommodate, if any? By filling out the preference page on eplans.com, we'll help you narrow your search.

At eplans.com we'll make the building process a snap to understand. At the click of a button you'll find a complete building guide. And our eplans task planner will create a construction calendar just for you. Here you'll find links to tips and other valuable information to help you every step of the way—from choosing a site to moving day.

For your added convenience, our home plans experts are available for live, one-on-one chats at eplans.com. Building a home may seem like a complicated project, but it doesn't have to be—particularly if you'll let us help you from start to finish.

HELPFUL BOOKS FROM **HOMEPLANNERS**

Order by phone 24 hours
1-800-322-6797
or visit our online bookstore at eplans.com

1 BIGGEST & BEST

1001 of our Best-Selling Plans
in One Volume.
1,074 to 7,275 square feet.
704 pgs. $12.95 IK1

2 ONE-STORY

450 designs for all lifestyles.
810 to 5,400 square feet.
448 pgs. $9.95 OS2

3 MORE ONE-STORY

475 Superb One-Level Plans
from 800 to 5,000
square feet.
448 pgs. $9.95 MO2

4 TWO-STORY

450 Best-Selling Designs
for 1½ and 2-stories.
448 pgs. $9.95 TS2

5 VACATION

430 designs for Recreation,
Retirement, and Leisure.
448 pgs. $9.95 VS3

6 HILLSIDE

208 designs for Split-Levels,
Bi-Levels, Multi-Levels,
and Walkouts.
224 pgs. $9.95 HH

7 FARMHOUSE

300 fresh designs from
Classic to Modern.
320 pgs. $10.95 FCP

8 COUNTRY HOUSES

208 unique home plans that
combine Traditional Style and
Modern Livability.
224 pgs. $9.95 CN

9 BUDGET-SMART

200 Efficient Plans from
7 Top Designers, that you can
really afford to build!
224 pgs. $8.95 BS

10 BARRIER-FREE

Over 1,700 products and
51 plans for Accessible Living.
128 pgs. $15.95 UH

11 ENCYCLOPEDIA

500 exceptional plans for all
styles and budgets—
The Best Book of its Kind!
528 pgs. $9.95 ENC3

12 SUN COUNTRY

175 Designs from
Coastal Cottages to
Stunning Southwesterns.
192 pgs. $9.95 SUN

13 AFFORDABLE

300 modest plans
for savvy homebuyers.
256 pgs. $9.95 AH2

14 VICTORIAN

210 striking Victorian and
Farmhouse designs from
today's top designers.
224 pgs. $15.95 VDH2

15 ESTATE

Dream big!
Eighteen designers showcase
their biggest and best plans.
224 pgs. $16.95 EDH3

16 LUXURY

170 lavish designs, over 50%
brand-new plans added to a
most elegant collection.
192 pgs. $12.95 LD3

17 WILLIAM E. POOLE

100 classic house plans from
William E. Poole.
224 pgs. $17.95 WP2

18 HUGE SELECTION

650 home plans—
from Cottages to Mansions
464 pgs. $8.95 650

19 SOUTHWEST

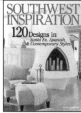

120 designs in Santa Fe,
Spanish, and
Contemporary Styles.
192 pgs. $14.95 SI

20 COUNTRY CLASSICS

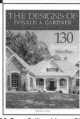

130 Best-Selling Home Plans
from Donald A. Gardner.
192 pgs. $17.95 DAG2

21 COTTAGES

245 Delightful retreats from
825 to 3,500 square feet.
256 pgs. $10.95 COOL

22 CONTEMPORARY

The most complete and
imaginative collection of
contemporary designs available.
256 pgs. $10.95 CM2

23 FRENCH COUNTRY

Live every day in the French
countryside using these plans,
landscapes and interiors.
192 pgs. $14.95 PN

24 SOUTHWESTERN

138 designs that capture the
spirit of the Southwest.
144 pgs. $10.95 SW

25 SHINGLE-STYLE

155 home plans from
Classic Colonials to
Breezy Bungalows.
192 pgs. $12.95 SNG

26 NEIGHBORHOOD

170 designs with the feel
of main street America.
192 pgs. $12.95 TND

27 CRAFTSMAN

170 Home plans in the
Craftsman and Bungalow
style. 192 pgs. $12.95 CC

28 GRAND VISTAS

200 Homes with a View.
224 pgs. $10.95 GV

29 MULTI-FAMILY

115 Duplex, Multiplex &
Townhome Designs.
128 pgs. $17.95 MFH

30 WATERFRONT

200 designs perfect for your
Waterside Wonderland.
208 pgs. $10.95 WF

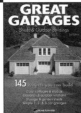

COPYRIGHT DOS & DON'TS

Blueprints for residential construction (or working drawings, as they are often called in the industry) are copyrighted intellectual property, protected under the terms of United States Copyright Law and, therefore, cannot be copied legally for use in building. However, we've made it easy for you to get what you need to build your home, without violating copyright law. Following are some guidelines to help you obtain the right number of copies for your chosen blueprint design.

COPYRIGHT DO

■ Do purchase enough copies of the blueprints to satisfy building requirements. As a rule for a home or project plan, you will need a set for yourself, two or three for your builder and subcontractors, two for the local building department, and one to three for your mortgage lender. You may want to check with your local building department or your builder to see how many they need before you purchase. You may need to buy eight to 10 sets; note that some areas of the country require purchase of vellums (also called reproducibles) instead of blueprints. Vellums can be written on and changed more easily than blueprints. Also, remember, plans are only good for one-time construction.

■ Do consider reverse blueprints if you want to flop the plan. Lettering and numbering will appear backward, but the reversed sets will help you and your builder better visualize the design.

■ Do take advantage of multiple-set discounts at the time you place your order. Usually, purchasing additional sets after you receive your initial order is not as cost-effective.

■ Do take advantage of vellums. Though they are a little more expensive, they can be changed, copied, and used for one-time construction of a home. You will receive a copyright release letter with your vellums that will allow you to have them copied.

■ Do talk with one of our professional service representatives before placing your order. They can give you great advice about what packages are available for your chosen design and what will work best for your particular situation.

COPYRIGHT DON'T

■ Don't think you should purchase only one set of blueprints for a building project. One is fine if you want to study the plan closely, but will not be enough for actual building.

■ Don't expect your builder or a copy center to make copies of standard blueprints. They cannot legally—most copy centers are aware of this.

■ Don't purchase standard blueprints if you know you'll want to make changes to the plans; vellums are a better value.

■ Don't use blueprints or vellums more than one time. Additional fees apply if you want to build more than one time from a set of drawings. ■

hanley ▲ wood
HomePlanners
ORDERING IS EASY

HANLEY WOOD HOMEPLANNERS HAS EVERYTHING YOU NEED TO BUILD THE home of your dreams, and with more than 50 years of experience in the industry, we make it as easy as possible for you to reach those goals. Just follow the steps on these pages and you'll receive a high-quality, ready-to-build set of home blueprints, plus everything else you need to make your home-building effort a success.

WHERE TO BEGIN?
1. CHOOSE YOUR PLAN

■ Browsing magazines, books, and eplans.com can be an exciting and rewarding part of the home-building process. As you search, make a list of the things you want in your dream home—everything from number of bedrooms and baths to details like fireplaces or a home office.

■ Take the time to consider your lot and your neighborhood, and how the home you choose will fit with both. And think about the future—how might your needs change if you plan to live in this house for five, 10, or 20 years?

■ With thousands of plans available, chances are that you'll have no trouble discovering your dream home. If you find something that's almost perfect, our Customization Program can help make it exactly what you want.

■ Most important, be sure to enjoy the process of picking out your new home!

WHAT YOU'LL GET WITH YOUR ORDER

Each designer's blueprint set is unique, but they all provide everything you'll need to build your home. Here are some standard elements you can expect to find in your plans:

1. FRONT PERSPECTIVE
This artist's sketch of the exterior of the house gives you an idea of how the house will look when built and landscaped.

2. FOUNDATION PLANS
This sheet shows the foundation layout including support walls, excavated and unexcavated areas, if any, and foundation notes. If your plan features slab construction rather than a basement, the plan shows footings and details for a monolithic slab. This page, or another in the set, may include a sample plot plan for locating your house on a building site.

3. DETAILED FLOOR PLANS
These plans show the layout of each floor of the house. Rooms and interior spaces are carefully dimensioned and keys are given for cross-section details provided later in the plans. The positions of electrical outlets and switches are shown.

4. HOUSE CROSS-SECTIONS
Large-scale views show sections or cutaways of the foundation, interior walls, exterior walls, floors, stairways, and roof details. Additional cross-sections may show important changes in floor, ceiling, or roof heights, or the relationship of one level to another. Extremely valuable during construction, these sections show exactly how the various parts of the house fit together.

5. INTERIOR ELEVATIONS
These elevations, or drawings, show the design and placement of kitchen and bathroom cabinets, laundry areas, fireplaces, bookcases, and other built-ins. Little extras, such as mantelpiece and wainscoting drawings, plus molding sections, provide details that give your home that custom touch.

6. EXTERIOR ELEVATIONS
Every blueprint set comes with drawings of the front exterior, and may include the rear and sides of your house as well. These drawings give necessary notes on exterior materials and finishes. Particular attention is given to cornice detail, brick, and stone accents or other finish items that make your home unique.

hanley▲wood
HomePlanners
ORDERING IS EASY

HANLEY WOOD
HOMEPLANNERS
ADVANTAGE
**ORDER
24 HOURS!**
1-800-521-6797

GETTING DOWN TO BUSINESS
2. PRICE YOUR PLAN

BLUEPRINT PRICE SCHEDULE

PRICE TIERS	1-SET STUDY PACKAGE	4-SET BUILDING PACKAGE	8-SET BUILDING PACKAGE	1-SET REPRODUCIBLE*
P1	$20	$50	$90	$140
P2	$40	$70	$110	$160
P3	$70	$100	$140	$190
P4	$100	$130	$170	$220
P5	$140	$170	$210	$270
P6	$180	$210	$250	$310
A1	$440	$490	$540	$660
A2	$480	$530	$580	$720
A3	$530	$590	$650	$800
A4	$575	$645	$705	$870
C1	$625	$695	$755	$935
C2	$670	$740	$800	$1000
C3	$715	$790	$855	$1075
C4	$765	$840	$905	$1150
L1	$870	$965	$1050	$1300
L2	$945	$1040	$1125	$1420
L3	$1050	$1150	$1240	$1575
L4	$1155	$1260	$1355	$1735
SQ1				.35/SQ. FT.

PRICES SUBJECT TO CHANGE

* REQUIRES A FAX NUMBER

plan #
READY TO ORDER

Once you've found your plan, get your plan number and turn to the following pages to find its price tier. Use the corresponding code and the Blueprint Price Schedule above to determine your price for a variety of blueprint packages.

Keep in mind that you'll need multiple sets to fulfill building requirements, and only reproducible sets may be altered or duplicated.

To the right you'll find prices for additional and reverse blueprint sets. Also note in the following pages whether your home has a corresponding Deck or Landscape Plan, and whether you can order our Quote One® cost-to-build information or a Materials List for your plan.

IT'S EASY TO ORDER
JUST VISIT
EPLANS.COM OR CALL
TOLL-FREE
1-800-521-6797

PRICE SCHEDULE FOR ADDITIONAL OPTIONS

OPTIONS FOR PLANS IN TIERS P1-P6	COSTS
ADDITIONAL IDENTICAL BLUEPRINTS FOR "P1-P6" PLANS	$10 PER SET
REVERSE BLUEPRINTS (MIRROR IMAGE) FOR "P1-P6" PLANS	$10 FEE PER ORDER
1 SET OF DECK CONSTRUCTION DETAILS	$14.95 EACH
DECK CONSTRUCTION PACKAGE (INCLUDES 1 OF "P1-P6" PLANS, PLUS 1 SET STANDARD DECK CONSTRUCTION DETAILS)	ADD $10 TO BUILDING PACKAGE PRICE

OPTIONS FOR PLANS IN TIERS A1-SQ1	COSTS
ADDITIONAL IDENTICAL BLUEPRINTS IN SAME ORDER FOR "A1-L4" PLANS	$50 PER SET
REVERSE BLUEPRINTS (MIRROR IMAGE) WITH 4- OR 8-SET ORDER FOR "A1-L4" PLANS	$50 FEE PER ORDER
SPECIFICATION OUTLINES	$10 EACH
MATERIALS LISTS FOR "A1-SQ1" PLANS	$70 EACH

IMPORTANT EXTRAS	COSTS
ELECTRICAL, PLUMBING, CONSTRUCTION, AND MECHANICAL DETAIL SETS	$14.95 EACH; ANY TWO $22.95; ANY THREE $29.95; ALL FOUR $39.95
HOME FURNITURE PLANNER	$15.95 EACH
REAR ELEVATION	$10 EACH
QUOTE ONE® SUMMARY COST REPORT	$29.95
QUOTE ONE® DETAILED COST ESTIMATE (FOR MORE DETAILS ABOUT QUOTE ONE®, SEE STEP 3.)	$60

IMPORTANT NOTE
Source Key
■ THE 1-SET STUDY PACKAGE IS MARKED "NOT FOR CONSTRUCTION."

HPK02

PLAN #	PRICE TIER	PAGE	MATERIALS LIST	QUOTE ONE®	DECK	DECK PRICE	LANDSCAPE	LANDSCAPE PRICE	REGIONS
HPK0200001	A3	8							
HPK0200002	L2	9							
HPK0200003	SQ1	10	Y						
HPK0200004	A4	11							
HPK0200005	C4	12							
HPK0200006	C2	13	Y						
HPK0200007	L1	14							
HPK0200008	SQ1	15							
HPK0200009	SQ1	16							
HPK0200010	SQ1	17	Y						
HPK0200011	L2	18							
HPK0200012	C1	19	Y	Y			OLA040	P4	123467
HPK0200013	SQ1	20							
HPK0200014	C2	21	Y						
HPK0200015	C1	22	Y						
HPK0200016	C4	23	Y						
HPK0200017	SQ1	24							
HPK0200018	SQ1	25							
HPK0200019	SQ1	26							
HPK0200020	A4	27	Y	Y					
HPK0200021	A4	28	Y						
HPK0200022	SQ1	29	Y						
HPK0200023	SQ1	30							
HPK0200024	A4	31	Y		ODA013	P2			
HPK0200025	A3	32	Y						
HPK0200026	A3	33	Y						
HPK0200027	A2	34	Y						
HPK0200028	C1	35	Y						
HPK0200029	A3	36	Y						
HPK0200030	A3	37							
HPK0200031	A3	38							
HPK0200032	A3	39							
HPK0200033	C3	40							
HPK0200034	C2	41							
HPK0200035	A4	42							
HPK0200036	A4	43							
HPK0200037	C4	44							
HPK0200038	A4	45	Y						
HPK0200039	A3	46							
HPK0200040	L1	47							
HPK0200041	C4	48							
HPK0200042	C1	49							
HPK0200043	A4	50							
HPK0200044	C1	51	Y						
HPK0200045	SQ1	52							
HPK0200046	SQ1	53							
HPK0200047	C1	54							
HPK0200048	A4	55							
HPK0200049	A3	56							
HPK0200050	C3	57							
HPK0200051	A3	58	Y				OLA004	P3	123568
HPK0200052	C1	59	Y						
HPK0200053	A4	60							
HPK0200054	L1	61							
HPK0200055	C1	62	Y						
HPK0200056	C2	63	Y						
HPK0200057	C1	64	Y						
HPK0200058	SQ1	65	Y						
HPK0200059	C3	66	Y						
HPK0200060	A2	67							
HPK0200061	A2	68							
HPK0200062	A2	69	Y						
HPK0200063	A2	70							
HPK0200064	A2	71	Y						
HPK0200065	A3	72	Y	Y			OLA004	P3	123568
HPK0200066	A2	73	Y						
HPK0200067	A3	74	Y						
HPK0200068	A2	75	Y						
HPK0200069	A2	76	Y						
HPK0200070	A3	77	Y						
HPK0200071	A3	78	Y	Y	ODA003	P2	OLA003	P3	123568
HPK0200072	A2	79	Y						
HPK0200073	A3	80	Y						
HPK0200074	A2	81	Y						
HPK0200075	A1	82	Y						
HPK0200076	C1	83	Y						
HPK0200077	A1	84	Y						
HPK0200078	A2	85	Y						
HPK0200079	A2	86	Y						
HPK0200080	A3	87	Y						
HPK0200081	A3	88	Y						
HPK0200082	A1	89	Y						
HPK0200083	A2	90	Y						
HPK0200084	A3	91	Y						
HPK0200085	A2	92	Y						
HPK0200086	A3	93	Y						
HPK0200087	A2	94	Y						
HPK0200088	C2	95	Y						
HPK0200089	A3	96	Y						
HPK0200090	A2	97	Y						
HPK0200091	A3	98	Y						
HPK0200092	A3	99	Y						
HPK0200093	C2	100							
HPK0200094	C1	101							
HPK0200095	A3	102	Y						
HPK0200096	A4	103	Y	Y					

ORDERING IS EASY

PLAN #	PRICE TIER	PAGE	MATERIALS LIST	QUOTE ONE®	DECK	DECK PRICE	LANDSCAPE	LANDSCAPE PRICE	REGIONS
HPK0200097	A3	104							
HPK0200098	A3	105							
HPK0200099	A3	106							
HPK0200100	C4	107	Y						
HPK0200101	C1	108							
HPK0200102	C1	109							
HPK0200103	C1	110							
HPK0200104	C2	111							
HPK0200105	A4	112	Y						
HPK0200106	C2	113	Y						
HPK0200107	A3	114	Y						
HPK0200108	C2	115	Y	Y	ODA012	P3	OLA084	P3	12345678
HPK0200109	A3	116	Y						
HPK0200110	A4	117	Y						
HPK0200111	C2	118	Y		ODA018	P3	OLA004	P3	123568
HPK0200112	A4	119	Y		ODA006	P2	OLA004	P3	123568
HPK0200113	A3	120							
HPK0200114	A3	121	Y						
HPK0200115	A3	122							
HPK0200116	C1	123							
HPK0200117	C1	124	Y						
HPK0200118	A3	125							
HPK0200119	C1	126	Y		ODA002	P2	OLA004	P3	123568
HPK0200120	C3	127	Y		ODA001	P2			
HPK0200121	C1	128							
HPK0200122	A3	129	Y						
HPK0200123	C1	130							
HPK0200124	C2	131							
HPK0200125	C1	132	Y		ODA013	P2	OLA002	P3	123568
HPK0200126	A4	133	Y	Y	ODA015	P2	OLA006	P3	123568
HPK0200127	C2	134							
HPK0200128	A4	135	Y						
HPK0200129	C1	136							
HPK0200130	C3	137	Y	Y			OLA003	P3	123568
HPK0200131	C1	138							
HPK0200132	C2	139							
HPK0200133	A2	140	Y		ODA004	P2	OLA003	P3	123568
HPK0200134	A3	141	Y	Y	ODA016	P2	OLA003	P3	123568
HPK0200135	A2	142	Y						
HPK0200136	C1	143	Y		ODA001	P2			
HPK0200137	C1	144							
HPK0200138	C2	145	Y		ODA018	P3			
HPK0200139	A2	146							
HPK0200140	A3	147							
HPK0200141	C3	148	Y	Y			OLA012	P3	12345678
HPK0200142	C2	149	Y	Y	ODA007	P3	OLA012	P3	12345678
HPK0200143	C1	150	Y		ODA015	P2	OLA011	P3	123568
HPK0200144	A3	151	Y		ODA015	P2	OLA004	P3	123568

PLAN #	PRICE TIER	PAGE	MATERIALS LIST	QUOTE ONE®	DECK	DECK PRICE	LANDSCAPE	LANDSCAPE PRICE	REGIONS
HPK0200145	A3	152	Y		ODA015	P2	OLA004	P3	123568
HPK0200146	A2	153	Y		ODA014	P2			
HPK0200147	A2	154	Y		ODA006	P2	OLA021	P3	123568
HPK0200148	A3	155							
HPK0200149	A3	156	Y	Y	ODA006	P2	OLA003	P3	123568
HPK0200150	C1	157	Y	Y					
HPK0200151	A4	158	Y		ODA016	P2	OLA001	P3	123568
HPK0200152	C4	159	Y	Y			OLA024	P4	123568
HPK0200153	SQ1	160							
HPK0200154	C4	161							
HPK0200155	L2	162							
HPK0200156	SQ1	163	Y						
HPK0200157	L2	164	Y						
HPK0200158	C4	165	Y				OLA008	P4	1234568
HPK0200159	SQ1	166	Y						
HPK0200160	SQ1	167	Y						
HPK0200161	SQ1	168	Y						
HPK0200162	SQ1	169							
HPK0200163	SQ1	170	Y						
HPK0200164	SQ1	171	Y						
HPK0200165	C4	172							
HPK0200166	C4	173							
HPK0200167	C3	174							
HPK0200168	C2	175							
HPK0200169	C3	176							
HPK0200170	C2	177							
HPK0200171	C2	178							
HPK0200172	C3	179							
HPK0200173	C1	180							
HPK0200174	L2	181							
HPK0200175	L1	182	Y						
HPK0200176	L2	183	Y						
HPK0200177	L2	184							
HPK0200178	L1	185							
HPK0200179	SQ1	186	Y						
HPK0200180	C3	187							
HPK0200181	SQ1	188							
HPK0200182	SQ1	189							
HPK0200183	L1	190							
HPK0200184	C4	191							
HPK0200185	L1	192	Y	Y	ODA008	P3	OLA016	P4	1234568
HPK0200186	C4	193							
HPK0200187	C3	194							
HPK0200188	C4	195							
HPK0200189	SQ1	196							

ORDER ONLINE AT EPLANS.COM

hanley▲wood
HomePlanners
ORDERING IS EASY

MORE TOOLS FOR SUCCESS
3. GET GREAT EXTRAS

WE OFFER A VARIETY OF USEFUL TOOLS THAT CAN HELP YOU THROUGH EVERY STEP OF THE home-building process. From our Materials List to our Customization Program, these items let you put our experience to work for you to ensure that you get exactly what you want out of your dream house.

MATERIALS LIST

For many of the designs in our portfolio, we offer a customized list of materials that helps you plan and estimate the cost of your new home. The Materials List outlines the quantity, type, and size of materials needed to build your house (with the exception of mechanical system items). Included are framing lumber, windows and doors, kitchen and bath cabinetry, rough and finished hardware, and much more. This handy list helps you or your builder cost out materials and serves as a reference sheet when you're compiling bids.

SPECIFICATION OUTLINE

This valuable 16-page document can play an important role in the construction of your house. Fill it in with your builder, and you'll have a step-by-step chronicle of 166 stages or items crucial to the building process. It provides a comprehensive review of the construction process and helps you choose materials.

QUOTE ONE®

The Quote One® system, which helps estimate the cost of building select designs in your zip code, is available in two parts: the Summary Cost Report and the Material Cost Report.

The Summary Cost Report, the first element in the package, breaks down the cost of your home into various categories based on building materials, labor, and installation, and includes three grades of construction: Budget, Standard, and Custom. Make even more informed decisions about your project with the second element of our package, the Material Cost Report. The material and installation cost is shown for each of more than 1,000 line items provided in the standard-grade Materials List, which is included with this tool. Additional space is included for estimates from contractors and subcontractors, such as for mechanical materials, which are not included in our packages.

If you are interested in a plan that does not indicate the availability of Quote One®, please call and ask our sales representatives, who can verify the status for you.

CUSTOMIZATION PROGRAM

If the plan you love needs something changed to make it perfect, our customization experts will ensure that you get nothing less than your dream home. Purchase a reproducible set of plans for the home you choose, and we'll send you our easy-to-use customization request form via e-mail or fax. For just $50, our customization experts will provide an estimate for your requested revisions, and once it's approved, that charge will be applied to your changes. You'll receive either five sets or a reproducible master of your modified design and any other options you select.

BUILDING BASICS

If you want to know more about building techniques—and deal more confidently with your subcontractors—we offer four useful detail sheets. These sheets provide non-plan-specific general information, but are excellent tools that will add to your understanding of Plumbing Details, Electrical Details, Construction Details, and Mechanical Details. These fact-filled sheets will help answer many of your building questions, and help you learn what questions to ask your builder and subcontractors.

GETTY IMAGES

hanley▲wood
HomePlanners

ORDERING IS EASY

ORDER 24 HOURS!
1-800-521-6797

HANDS-ON HOME FURNITURE PLANNER

Effectively plan the space in your home using our Hands-On Home Furniture Planner. It's fun and easy—no more moving heavy pieces of furniture to see how the room will go together. The kit includes reusable peel-and-stick furniture templates that fit on a 12"x18" laminated layout board—enough space to lay out every room in your house.

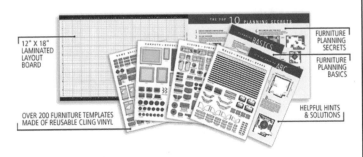

12" X 18" LAMINATED LAYOUT BOARD

FURNITURE PLANNING SECRETS

FURNITURE PLANNING BASICS

HELPFUL HINTS & SOLUTIONS

OVER 200 FURNITURE TEMPLATES MADE OF REUSABLE CLING VINYL

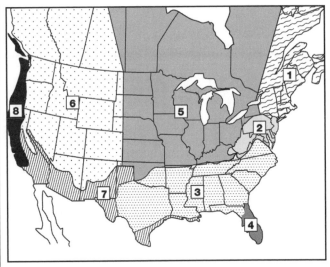

DECK BLUEPRINT PACKAGE

Many of the homes in this book can be enhanced with a professionally designed Home Planners Deck Plan. Those plans marked with a **D** have a corresponding deck plan, sold separately, which includes a Deck Plan Frontal Sheet, Deck Framing and Floor Plans, Deck Elevations, and a Deck Materials List. A Standard Deck Details Package, also available, provides all the how-to information necessary for building any deck. Get both the Deck Plan and the Standard Deck Details Package for one low price in our Complete Deck Building Package.

LANDSCAPE BLUEPRINT PACKAGE

Homes marked with an **L** in this book have a front-yard Landscape Plan that is complementary in design to the house plan. These comprehensive Landscape Blueprint Packages include a Frontal Sheet, Plan View, Regionalized Plant & Materials List, a sheet on Planting and Maintaining Your Landscape, Zone Maps, and a Plant Size and Description Guide. Each set of blueprints is a full 18" x 24" with clear, complete instructions in easy-to-read type.

Our Landscape Plans are available with a Plant & Materials List adapted by horticultural experts to eight regions of the country. Please specify from the following regions when ordering your plan:

Region 1: Northeast
Region 2: Mid-Atlantic
Region 3: Deep South
Region 4: Florida & Gulf Coast
Region 5: Midwest
Region 6: Rocky Mountains
Region 7: Southern California & Desert Southwest
Region 8: Northern California & Pacific Northwest

OUR EXCHANGE POLICY

With the exception of reproducible plan orders, we will exchange your entire first order for an equal or greater number of blueprints within our plan collection within **60 days** of the original order. The entire content of your original order must be returned before an exchange will be processed. Please call our customer service department at 1-888-690-1116 for your return authorization number and shipping instructions. If the returned blueprints look used, redlined, or copied, we will not honor your exchange. Fees for exchanging your blueprints are as follows: 20% of the amount of the original order, plus the difference in cost if exchanging for a design in a higher price bracket or less the difference in cost if exchanging for a design in a lower price bracket. (Reproducible blueprints are not exchangeable or refundable.) Please call for current postage and handling prices. Shipping and handling charges are not refundable.

ABOUT REPRODUCIBLES

Reproducibles (often called "vellums") are the most convenient way to order your blueprints. In any building process, you will need multiple copies of your blueprints for your builder, subcontractors, lenders, and the local building department. In addition, you may want or need to make changes to the original design. Such changes should be made only by a licensed architect or engineer. When you purchase reproducibles, you will receive a copyright release letter that allows you to have them altered and copied. You will want to purchase a reproducible plan if you plan to make any changes, whether by using our convenient Customization Program or going to a local architect.

ABOUT REVERSE BLUEPRINTS

Although lettering and dimensions will appear backward, reverses will be a useful aid if you decide to flop the plan. See Price Schedule and Plans Index for pricing.

ARCHITECTURAL AND ENGINEERING SEALS

Some cities and states now require that a licensed architect or engineer review and "seal" a blueprint, or officially approve it, prior to construction. Prior to application for a building permit or the start of actual construction, we strongly advise that you consult your local building official who can tell you if such a review is required.

ABOUT THE DESIGNS

The architects and designers whose work appears in this publication are among America's leading residential designers. Each plan was designed to meet the requirements of a nationally recognized model building code in effect at the time and place the plan was drawn. Because national building codes change from time to time, plans may not fully comply with any such code at the time they are sold to a customer. In addition, building officials may not accept these plans as final construction documents of record as the plans may need to be modified and additional drawings and details added to suit local conditions and requirements. Purchasers should consult a licensed architect or engineer, and their local building official, before starting any construction related to these plans.

LOCAL BUILDING CODES AND ZONING REQUIREMENTS

At the time of creation, these plans are drawn to specifications published by the Building Officials and Code Administrators (BOCA) International, Inc.; the Southern Building Code Congress International, (SBCCI) Inc.; the International Conference of Building Officials (ICBO); or the Council of American Building Officials (CABO). These plans are designed to meet or exceed national building standards. Because of the great differences in geography and climate throughout the United States and Canada, each state, county, and municipality has its own building codes, zone requirements, ordinances, and building regulations. Your plan may need to be modified to comply with local requirements. In addition, you may need to obtain permits or inspections from local governments before and in the course of construction. We authorize the use of the blueprints on the express condition that you consult a local licensed architect or engineer of your choice prior to beginning construction and strictly comply with all local building codes, zoning requirements, and other applicable laws, regulations, ordinances, and requirements. Notice: Plans for homes to be built in Nevada must be redrawn by a Nevada-registered professional. Consult your building official for more information on this subject.

TERMS AND CONDITIONS

These designs are protected under the terms of United States Copyright Law and may not be copied or reproduced in any way, by any means, unless you have purchased reproducibles which clearly indicate your right to copy or reproduce. We authorize the use of your chosen design as an aid in the construction of one single- or multi-family home only. You may not use this design to build a second or multiple dwellings without purchasing another blueprint or blueprints or paying additional design fees.

HOW MANY BLUEPRINTS DO YOU NEED?

Although a four-set building package may satisfy many states, cities, and counties, some plans may require certain changes. For your convenience, we have developed a reproducible plan, which allows you to take advantage of our Customization Program, or to have a local professional modify and make up to 10 copies of your revised plan. As our plans are all copyright protected, with your purchase of the reproducible, we will supply you with a copyright release letter. The number of copies you may need: 1 for owner, 3 for builder, 2 for local building department, and 1-3 sets for your mortgage lender.

DISCLAIMER

The designers we work with have put substantial care and effort into the creation of their blueprints. However, because we cannot provide on-site consultation, supervision, and control over actual construction, and because of the great variance in local building requirements, building practices, and soil, seismic, weather, and other conditions, **WE MAKE NO WARRANTY OF ANY KIND, EXPRESS OR IMPLIED, WITH RESPECT TO THE CONTENT OR USE OF THE BLUEPRINTS, INCLUDING BUT NOT LIMITED TO ANY WARRANTY OF MERCHANTABILITY OR OF FITNESS FOR A PARTICULAR PURPOSE. ITEMS, PRICES, TERMS, AND CONDITIONS ARE SUBJECT TO CHANGE WITHOUT NOTICE.**

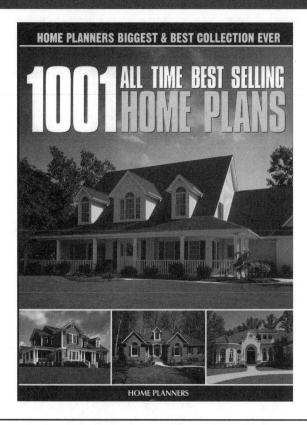
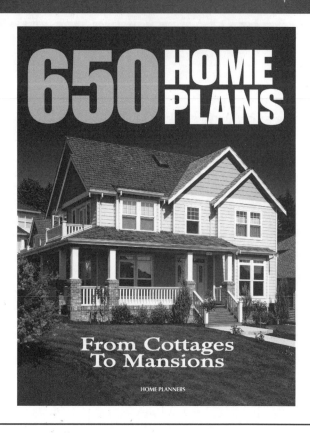
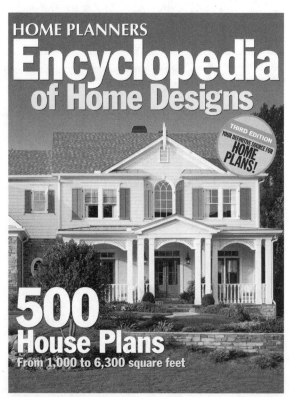